Praise for *Daddy's Little Stranger*

"Acamea Deadwiler's *Daddy's Little Stranger* is a powerful and deeply felt memoir of family, longing, estrangement, complicated love, and what ties us to ourselves. Deadwiler's writing is stunningly intimate, reflective, and honest. From childhood to adulthood, *Daddy's Little Stranger* searches for connection, replete with pink Reeboks and #GirlDad tags. Deadwiler's book curled up in my heart and soothed me in my own fatherless, daughterly ache, whispering "it's okay." I loved every tender moment of this memoir and I know you will too."
— Jane Wong, author of *Meet Me Tonight in Atlantic City*

"From the opening heartbreaking chapter to its final poignant pages, Acamea Deadwiler's *Daddy's Little Stranger* artfully demonstrates a simple but often overlooked fact: memoir never simply reproduces the past. Rather, it brings the past to life by exploring our relationship to memory itself. *Daddy's Little Stranger* does not follow the familiar, triumphal storyline of overcoming difficult circumstances by refusing to be broken by them. Through masterful prose, keen observation, and vulnerable self-reflection, Deadwiler finds narrative balance, reconciling the pain of her childhood and offering the reader the greatest gift that art has to offer: wisdom."
— Jeremy Schraffenberger, Editor, *North American Review*

"Daddy's Little Stranger is a piercing and powerful exploration of an emotional landscape shaped by a father's absence. Acamea Deadwiler's page-turner memoir grapples with grit, growth, loss, and human imperfection. It's also a testament to the transformative potential of storytelling."

    – Danielle Ofri, Editor, *Bellevue Literary Review*, and author of
    What Doctors Feel: How Emotions Affect the Practice of Medicine

"In *Daddy's Little Stranger*, Acamea Deadwiler offers readers an honest, yet hopeful self-portrait of adolescent resilience, adaptation and courage. As she reconciles grief, loss and betrayal caused by physically and emotionally absent parents, Deadwiler's intimate narrative quietly reveals her self-preservation and determination. While skillfully presenting an adult consciousness, Deadwiler also remains graciously loyal to the voice of her younger self and the healing of her inner child. Daddy's Little Stranger is an inspirational testimony for all of us who want to believe that the traumas of our past do not dictate the daughters we become."

    – Daria Peoples, author and illustrator of *Hello, Mister Blue*

Daddy's Little Stranger

Acamea Deadwiler

Riddle Brook Publishing
Peterborough, NH

CIP data available from the publisher.

Library of Congress Control Number: 2024930210
ISBN (Trade Paper): 979-8-9859413-8-8
ISBN (EPUB): 979-8-9859413-9-5

Cover image © 2024 by Mary Ann Reilly
Cover design by Nebojsa

Riddle Brook Publishing, LLC
Peterborough, NH
www.riddlebrookpublishing.com

Dedicated to my mother,
who it feels like I'm seeing for the first time.

Contents

1

The Formula

I made sure to adorn my feet with the low-top, aerobic-style pink Reeboks my father bought me when we were last together. The sneakers were proof that he loved me. Maybe he'd see me wearing them and remember.

I thought when he came to get me, I might extend my leg forward, tilt my foot back on its heel, and call attention to the Reeboks. "Look Daddy," I'd smile and say. He'd smile back, delighted I weighed more heavily his best deed than the months since passed. He'd recall being the father some part of him hoped to be, and perhaps wish to be that father again.

A tan, floral-patterned armchair sat in front of our living room window. I climbed atop it and waited on my knees for the man whose mother calls him "Champ." *Champ.* I giggled. Saying it to myself with a hard *p* was amusing. *Champ-ah.*

White metal bars outside the window were rusting. It seemed to happen in real-time. As though paint was peeling, drifting to the ground while I glared through the spaces between.

Our one-story white house with yellow trim was first, or last, on the block depending on which direction you were traveling. My eyes widened with every car that rounded the corner, hoping to find my father behind the wheel. I didn't know what he'd be driving. I could only wait to see if the oncoming sedan, coupe, or minivan stopped at our address.

I found a new rust spot every time I alternated to the bars from staring at an oil spill in the driveway. Then my attention darted out toward the sound of approaching vehicles. Back to the street, back to the circle of oil in the driveway, back to a freshly revealed rust spot.

Pink Reeboks and folded lace-trimmed socks dangled over the chair's edge. "This is my daughter," I heard in my mind as though the accompanying scene had occurred more recently. When Champ took me to The Village to get the sneakers, he said this to the lady who helped us. Joy rocketed through my body. I squeezed his thick index finger a little tighter and looked up at the side of his stubbled face before nodding in agreement at the saleslady.

Champ did know he was my father. I often wondered. Because where was he all this time he hadn't been with me? I wondered if Mommy also turned everything he believed about the matter upside down. Had she shaken the contents of his universe empty like she'd done mine?

An apology rested on my tongue, but I didn't find the courage to set it free. Did Champ know until, and even now, that another man had declared himself my daddy? I wanted him to understand I only complied because I knew no better.

For the first five or so years of my existence, as early as I was able to form beliefs, I believed my brother Danny and I shared a father. We called him "Daddy," always, and being twenty months the elder, Daddy was mine first. *Mine* before he was *ours*. Mine until my mother sat me down and explained her high school boyfriend was my real father. Then I realized Daddy wasn't mine at all. Not in the way I'd held him to be.

Still, the dots didn't completely connect inside my brain.

Daddy didn't belong to me?

But, how, when I called him by this name?

My mother didn't need to map out the entire journey for me to grasp that we'd arrived at its end. I was no longer Daddy's daughter. Another man came to claim me. To fill my heart before it could break, I focused not on the lost father, but on the one I'd gained. I was all in on this mystery person.

After Champ and I had left Foot Locker with my new shoes, we walked past boutiques and vacant spaces where stores should have been until we got to everyone's favorite spot in the strip mall, Chuck Wheeler's Vienna Beef Red Hots. They made the best hot dogs and Polish sausages not just in Gary, Indiana, but the entire region. At least according to my aunts and uncles.

"What do you want on your hot dog?" Champ asked.

"Just ketchup!"

He looked pleasantly perplexed, squinting his eyes and half-smiling, like he'd discovered some interesting secret about me. I didn't want to ruin the flavor of my hot dog, the best hot dog, by smothering it in relish, onions, or mustard the way I saw most other people do. Champ shrugged at the lady working the register. "And gimme one with just ketchup."

We walked toward the exit shoving food into our faces and slurping grape-flavored Crush. Our mouths were full, leaving no space for words we might have searched to find. Champ finished his hot dog before we even got to the parking lot. I was careful not to make a mess while finishing my last few bites inside the car.

I'd worn a subtle grin the entire drive back to my house, watching Champ smoke cigarette after cigarette and fiddle with the car stereo. The ashtray was overflowing, yet he kept stuffing in more Newport butts. It seemed like he still didn't know what to say, only asking if I was "okay" every few minutes. I offered a reassuring "mmhmm" in return.

Everything was perfect. About ninety minutes is all that was required to make me see myself as a daughter with a dad, again. Ninety minutes, after five years of not knowing this dad existed, and three where his intermittent visits left room to forget.

The Village outing was months ago. I wondered if Champ had changed his mind. Had I done something wrong? Was I not the daughter he'd imagined I'd be? I remembered Foot Locker, the saleslady, the confirmation, and I knew he knew. So, what was it that prevented my father from choosing me? Not all the time. Just, a few more times. That would be enough.

I was waiting in front of the window because I'd taken matters into my own hands. Because school was restarting the next day. My need for a backpack seemed as great an excuse as any to call my father. Maybe we could go back to The Village and buy one, and he'd recall how I like my hot dogs.

Mommy had gotten me ready for the day. She delighted in dressing me up to look pretty. She's crafty and resourceful, good at piecing things together. No one would ever catch me looking a mess or her allowing it to happen.

You should've seen me on Sundays. She went all out for church. Sometimes her stylings were too fancy for my taste with ribbons and bows, shimmery stockings, and patent leather shoes. I had a closet full of white and pastel-colored dresses my wealthy aunt brought whenever she visited from Chicago. Most had ruffles. Some had puffy sleeves or matching satin gloves. Mommy made her picks every week based on the occasion. If it were a holiday service, oh boy. She'd pull out all the stops. Because I'd always have a speech to recite in front of the congregation, I might've been in ruffles and gloves and puffy sleeves, and a hat.

I'd stay up late the night before Christmas or Easter services, going over my speech with Grandma. For someone who didn't show much emotion, she reveled in the art of theatrics. She'd tell me when to look sad or amazed and how to make my delivery more "enchanting." This was our bonding time. My opportunity to demonstrate my worth. "Again!" Grandma would order. Again. Again. As many times as it took to satisfy her.

Washington Street Church of God was a massive three-level structure. A clock hung against the front edge of the balcony. I'd clutch a microphone in my right, white-gloved hand when Sunday came, turn toward the clock and let my speech rip with a confident cadence. Though poised, my voice was small and soft, a byproduct of not being allowed to use it often. But assertiveness swelled beneath my tone when performing.

I raised my pitch at the end of one speech, just as I announced how Mary Magdalene found Jesus' tomb empty. "He is Risen!" echoed through the sanctuary speakers. I paused for dramatic effect, looking up at the sky as though I'd discovered the empty tomb myself. The audience erupted with cheers, moving to its feet in unanimous applause.

"Amen!"

"Praise God!"

"Hallelujah!"

"That's alright, Miss Camey!"

I passed the mic back to the smiling emcee and returned to my seat, expressionless. Pleased, but aware I hadn't done anything special. I did what I was supposed to do. What I'd been trained to do. Be perfect. Impeccable performance was my means to an end—assurance I was loved, or at least lovable, or at worst tolerable.

After the service, when church ladies would come over to tell me how great a job I had done, they'd also compliment me and Mommy on my outfit. "That dress is *beauuutiful*," they'd say while spinning me around to get a good look. I thought the praise made Mommy proud. She'd smile and give them all the details on how she'd put the ensemble together. I imagined it a small victory she held to balance against the side of her heart's scale burdened with times she may have fallen short. Never had she dropped the ball on my fashion. At this, she was mother of the year, every year.

In preparing me for my father, however, Mommy kept it simple. After cleaning my face, she ironed one of my nicest short sets to match the pink Reeboks. She did my hair into banana-curled pigtails, my signature style. I looked the part of a princess any father would be honored to claim. But the perfection-equals-love formula didn't seem to work on mine.

I was ready to run out of the house before the early afternoon time Champ designated. I didn't want him to wait long. It was my pleasure to sit, primed for his arrival.

A car barreled down the block. I sat up straight and pushed my face into the window. My fingers gripped the top of the chair. Before I could get a good look at the car, it was out of sight. Enthusiasm rocked my body back and forth as cars kept right on going past our house. It was like the night before Christmas, when you lie in bed unable to sleep because you can't wait to see what the morning will bring. I couldn't rest.

My heart pounded faster when a vehicle neared. The thumping felt too big for my body. I might've been shaking. Might've been humming a made-up melody. I was so eager and anxious I almost couldn't stand it. Only my will kept me from hopping down from the chair and sprinting circles around the living room.

White paint chips were now speckled across the flower bed below our window, next to the front porch. Sixteen . . . Seventeen . . . Ninete—wait. One . . . Two . . . I lost my place while counting the speckles until I got tired of starting over. There was a tiny metal fence protecting the flower bed from footsteps and errant objects. I counted the holes in the fence instead.

Kids rode their bikes up, down, and around the block. Each instance the same boy or girl zipped past, the sky was a bit duller. Then one by one, kids stopped returning. Many of the youngsters I saw frolicking across the street gathered their toys and headed into their houses. The remaining few continued wrestling in their front yards or shooting a near-deflated basketball into the milk crate posted above a garage. Soon, they too disappeared behind their front doors.

Parents emerged from homes and moved their vehicles from the curb into the driveways their children had used as playing surfaces. The sight and smell of smoke rising from barbecue grills dissipated. Music stopped. Porch lights flicked on. I watched the block come to life, and I watched it die. How could the day have ended for so many before mine began? Maybe my day was ending too.

Tears were waiting. The orange sun dipped into my line of blurring sight. Since I'd only paid fleeting attention to its retreat, it seemed to set all at once. The sky turned black. Some part of me knew the likelihood of my father arriving decreased with the departure of daylight. The idea squeezed air from my lungs. It filled my eyelids with the water I refused to let fall.

I will not cry. I will not cry. I will not cry.

They couldn't see me cry, my mother and brother. I was already embarrassed they'd seen me staring out of the window all day. ALL DAY. They saw me sitting there sporting one of my best outfits. Smiling like a dummy. Behaving as though someone who came for me just twice in eight years might come for me again. I was embarrassed because they knew. Both had begged me to watch TV or read a book until my father arrived. I'd shunned them, scoffed at their suggestions.

Mommy, no match for my defiance, had tried a couple of

times to coax me down from the chair before retreating to her room. Danny had invited me to play games with him. "Why are you just sitting there?" he asked. He didn't understand. His father always came for him. He came for me too. Danny thought this should've been sufficient and was baffled by my desperate demonstration of longing for this new Daddy.

But if I hadn't sat and watched, I'd have sworn Champ came and we just didn't hear the car horn or his knock on the door. Or I would've convinced myself he'd gotten lost and passed our house a few times, uncertain if it was ours. I would have believed he'd sat in the driveway waiting, assumed I wasn't ready, and left. So dead smack in front of the window I remained. Now, here I was, foolishly peering out into darkness. Refusing to concede defeat, still.

Giving up would've let the two doubters win. I wanted my father to come through in the clutch. To arrive in the eleventh hour and rush to the front door with a grand reason for his flagrant tardiness. I wanted him to show everyone I was right to wait. I'd flash them a victorious smirk when he retrieved me. I'd yell "See!" as though certain I'd soon be rescued from this disaster of a day. My sibling and our mother would nod in apologetic surrender as my father took my hand in his and whisked me away.

Because I wanted the scene to unfold with everything inside me and it had not, because I was dismissive and baselessly cocky in my belief, I was embarrassed. Releasing my tears would only compound the humiliation. I knew there would be no consoling hugs. We weren't that kind of family. There would be emotional avoidance from my mother and something to the effect of "I told you so" from a brother who didn't yet know what not to say. I couldn't allow this inevitable event to occur and could not cry because there would be no comfort.

I needed my person to take his rightful place. *My* person,

who, while I defiantly guarded his name, was busy letting me down. But he'll come. He's coming. I kept feeding myself the idea because I couldn't bear to accept otherwise.

I did not rise. I did not relent and withdraw to my room. Propped up on my knees, I rested my chin on the back of the chair. My shoulders sank and though my gaze fell, it remained fixed on the shadowy street. I pleaded in silence for Champ to show up, bargaining with whatever god might hear for the next car to be his.

I'll do what Mommy says. I'll get all satisfactory marks on my report card. I'll keep my room clean.

These were all things I did anyway. I only hoped the formal offering might be accepted in exchange for the fulfillment of my most urgent desire. What had I done to be denied?

That my father didn't want me enough to preserve the space he vowed to save for us, pushed me past shame. I was a good girl and an honor roll student who didn't give anyone any trouble. I was everything I'd promised to be, and it was insufficient. I didn't know what more I could become that might've lifted me to a level of relevance in his life.

It's my fault. I shouldn't have asked him to come. Because maybe he didn't want to.

I should have waited for him to come on his own. Things turned out better when it was his idea. I had to push, and in doing so, set him up to fail.

I wished I could start over, tell him "I'm sorry" and that I would wait for his return as long as he'd like if it meant he would one day return. That's what a perfect daughter would do. She wouldn't force the issue or make her father feel incompetent.

A car turned into the driveway. I'd long lost the energy to summon excitement, but I hoped.

I continued doing what I'd done all day. Staring. I watched the car inch further into visibility, arousing faint optimism.

It's him . . .
It's him . . .
It's not.
And it never will be again.

2

I Remember

I miss the years before Champ entered my life only to break it. Because in those days, I had a doting Daddy. Danny's father held me and danced with me, and by him I knew for sure I was loved. Loving him in return, calling him *Daddy* was easy until I learned of my own father and no longer knew what to name him.

Daddy seemed *giant*. He was tall and chocolate, with huge arms inside of which I felt safe, shielded from anything or anyone who might dare bring harm. Thick, square, brown-rimmed glasses sat on the tip of his nose, surrounded by a mostly smooth, hairless face.

In his white sailor outfit, complete with round hat and black neckerchief, Daddy looked like he'd stepped out of a war movie. People saluted and nodded at him when we walked through stores. Anywhere he wore the uniform, folks went out of their way to greet him. With my hand in his I'd look up, anticipating a reaction when strangers shared their gratitude for his service.

It felt like I was with a celebrity, one I was fortunate to also have as my Daddy. The attention didn't faze him much. He offered admirers a quick head bow and kept it moving. Those who were especially cheerful could sometimes get him to crack an almost-smile. But that was it. He wasn't much for the spotlight, and wore his stoic military face out in the world. It was cool though, watching people appreciate him. I soaked up enough of the attention for both of us.

My mother married Daddy when I was too young to know it. In my mind, he was always there. We'd always loved each other. He was different with me than with strangers. I got to see him laugh and be silly. When he tickled my belly and boosted me up onto his shoulders in the middle of carnival crowds, I forgot he was a sailor at all. I think he did too. In those moments, no fate but mine rested in his hands.

When I was set to start kindergarten, the Navy stationed Daddy in San Diego and off we went from Indiana to California. We moved into an apartment complex with other military families. There were hills of grass in the front and a canyon in the back. The door to our unit was red. It opened to reveal slick hardwood floors Danny and I slid across in our socks, crashing into walls and each other. We had fun in our new place. The red door though . . . for years I would see it in my nightmares.

I would see the door on fire. Sometimes I'd dream the red paint was blood. Or, I'd be running from something, trying to get away only to yank on the door and have it not open. Sometimes, the sight of the red door alone was enough to jar me awake. Until then, I thought the colorful door was pretty and we were a happy little four-person family behind it.

I hated when anyone was upset with me, but especially Daddy. Once, excited to show him a picture I'd drawn, I barged into my parents' bedroom without knocking. I wasn't exactly sure what I saw but knew I shouldn't have seen it. I froze in the doorway at the sight of Daddy's naked body.

He yelled, "Get out!" Daddy rarely raised his voice around me, let alone at me. On the occasions he did, it felt like the force punched a hole through my chest. I quickly shut the door and ran sniffling into my room.

While my tears dried, I grabbed my crayons and a piece of paper. In colorful crooked letters, I scrawled "I'm sorry" next to stick-figure representations of me and Daddy holding hands. Pleased with my work, I tiptoed back down the hall, slid the creation under my parents' door, and scurried away.

A few minutes later, as I sat on my bed making more drawings, Daddy walked into the room. He didn't say anything, only lifted me into those strong arms and smiled. He hugged the doubt and anxiety out of my body and carried me into the living room. We were still best friends. That was always all I needed to know. He still loved me when I messed up or did something wrong. I didn't need to be perfect for Daddy.

Mere months into our California life, however, things fell apart. Behind the scenes of my mother's marriage were varying forms of domestic abuse and deteriorating mental health. There was control masquerading as devotion. Soon, it pushed my mother past her breaking point. While Daddy was away on military assignment, her mind went to a place miles away from reality. She wasn't in the same world with us anymore, forget the same room.

I'm sure there were small signs I missed. Blips in behavior my young mind didn't pick up on or register as alarming. I remember she grew restless and distracted when awake, bouncing from one unfinished task to another. She worked frantically on menial projects like washing walls, only to do an about face and leave the job undone. A sopping wet rag rested on the hardwood floor next to a bucket of soapy water, both abandoned.

Maybe my mother also said something unusual, slept into the afternoons, or didn't sleep much at all in the beginning. She might've claimed to hear something no one else heard. Maybe she put the milk in a cabinet or left water running in the bathtub until it overflowed. There must've been preceding cracks in her foundation, but mostly, I only remember the crumbling.

I remember the day we got our first major sign something was wrong. Danny and I sat anticipating what turned out to be the last meal our mother prepared for us in the apartment. It was Quaker Oats. The air was warm with a sweet, spicy aroma that let me know she'd added cinnamon and raisins, just how I liked it.

Danny and I launched into our usual time-to-eat chair dance with shoulders shimmying and heads bobbing. We stopped mid-bop when our mother emerged from the kitchen to fill our bowls with oatmeal. A metal spoon clanked against the pot as she stirred. But a step from the table, the stirring ceased. My mother's body went stiff, and her face went blank. She fixed her gaze inside the pot as though something there didn't belong.

My eyes lifted to meet hers. I half-feared something was wrong, half-waited for her to distribute the oatmeal, too hungry for complete concern. My eyes followed her as she walked back into the kitchen, then to the trash where she dumped all the oatmeal. I watched her open our refrigerator and scan its contents before grabbing an armful. She paced between the refrigerator and the garbage, tossing more and more items into the trash with the fervor of a person carrying out an urgent mission. Back and forth she went, explaining that "they" had poisoned our food.

My lip quivered watching her, spoon still clutched in my fist. Danny and I stared at our mother, awaiting further instruction. We stared at each other when those instructions did not come.

We stared at the covered windows, at the slices of California sunshine forcing entry into our asylum.

The windows were concealed behind drawn blinds and pulled shades, our mother cocooning us inside a new universe, shielding us from spies attempting to watch us from the canyon. For double protection, after throwing out our food, she instructed us to stay below the windowsills to ensure we remained hidden. Most hours of every day forward, the three of us crouched or laid atop couch cushions she'd tossed to the floor after announcing that the hardwood was contaminated. She told us we couldn't touch its surface for a second without absorbing poison.

I remember how everything seemed an adventure in the beginning. An endless living room slumber party where we came up with clever ways to avoid outside detection and rode my mother's slight frame around the apartment. When Danny or I needed to use the bathroom, she got on all fours and had us mount her back. She carried us, one at a time, to and from the toilet. It was like a pony ride.

We had to be extra still and quiet when Cee-Cee knocked on the red door. She was my neighbor and best friend who came by daily to see if I could play outside. Cee-Cee was Hawaiian. She had long black hair draped past her waist. Her mom did too.

The two of us would talk about missing our daddies while they were away. I enjoyed guessing when they might return, and firing off questions about Cee-Cee's native island. But now we couldn't risk opening our front door with looming danger on the other side. When she knocked, I melted into the cushions, making myself invisible until she gave up hope and left.

As our mother slept more, aching bellies made my brother and me defy her orders. We believed everything she told us but took our chances, more famished than afraid. The hunger was a certainty. We could feel it twisting our insides, digging a cave through our guts. Warnings from our mother were scary, but only ideas. All we had as confirmation were her words. The hunger was a clear and present menace.

Danny and I scooted to the edge of the couch cushions and touched our toes to the hardwood as though testing the temperature of water. First, big toe. Then the other four toes. Finally, a heel. Nothing happened. We thought maybe the poison took time to work, but *now* was all that mattered. It seemed safe to plant both feet on the floor and stand.

I remember. We tiptoed around the apartment during secret survival sessions, the balls of our bare feet causing a faint tap with every quick step. Each time we did this without dying, we grew less afraid to do it again. First stop was the kitchen. My mother must've gotten distracted again while disposing of our poisoned food, because inside the refrigerator was an open package of hot dogs and another containing several slices of bacon. The way those two items sat alone on a shelf made the refrigerator seem barer than if we'd found nothing.

Both of us grabbed a hot dog and ate it raw. It was fascinating how the wieners didn't taste much different than when boiled. After a day or two we'd emptied the package and started in on the bacon. The slices were white and waxy, nowhere near what Mommy served from the skillet. We could tell it needed to be cooked, and spread slices across a warm heating vent. It felt like an eternity passed before each piece began to warm and slowly curl into a light shade of pink. Holding back longer than the minutes it took for this slight transformation seemed impossible. Danny and I peeled strips from the vent and stuffed greasy, chewy fistfuls into our tiny mouths.

Sometimes, Mommy opened her eyes and scratched out a soft, "What are you doing?" Without ever waiting for an answer, she'd tell us to come back and sit down. We didn't obey once we realized most of the time, even if looking in our direction, she didn't see us. She was watching something beyond the realm of our existence. Only now and then did her awareness snap back to her children.

After our rebellious hot dog eating and bacon warming, sneaking around the apartment ended with taking turns atop our little bathroom stool, drinking water from the faucet. Once done, we returned to our place on the couch cushions and resumed watching *The Care Bears Movie* as though we'd been there all along. By now we could recite the lines word-for-word. Something about the familiarity brought us comfort. It tethered us to reality. If the movie was playing, we knew we were still here.

Danny and I could have drawn this routine out longer if we were smarter with the limited food rations. Instead, we showed minimal restraint, not considering this might continue longer than it had or what we might do once there was nothing left to eat. When the bacon ran out, so did our ideas. At five and four years old, we'd reached the limits of both our bravery and creativity.

I remember waiting. With pride and confidence, I waited for Daddy to come rescue us. He would handle the bad guys who did the mean things and made us captives in our home. I expected him to return, come through the door with McDonald's Chicken McNuggets and make everything better. Because that's what heroes do and mine never failed me.

When the voices of Grumpy Bear and Cheer Bear faded into the background, it was already too late. Hunger surpassed its pain. Our bodies fell, too weak to send distress signals, as organs shifted from fight, to flight, to surrender. Without the energy to even fuel aching, we slept next to our mother. The three of us coiled against one another, huddled at the feet of mercy.

Creeping away from the designated safe area ended. Assisted trips to the bathroom were less exciting. Mommy moved slower. Her knees made little squeaks as they dragged across the polished hardwood. I could barely stay upright for the rides and mustered only sluggish sliding dismounts from her back to a slumped position on the toilet. She lowered her body to the ground, waiting to haul me back to our cushions once finished. We returned and collapsed into a heap.

It always felt like night.

I see us at day three without food, or maybe it was day four, or day fourteen. The days bled into each other. The passage of hours was marked only by altered states and increasing stages of weakness. Everything looked fuzzy. My legs wobbled when I tried to use them. Moving my body at all felt like a task I was not adequately equipped to perform, so I stopped trying. Though trying would have proven futile. I would say I gave up, but the phrase implies a choice. My limbs and senses were overwhelmed into submission.

The Care Bears Movie ended again and no one went to the VCR to hit rewind and play this time. A blank TV screen watched over us. No one flushed the toilet, flipped a light switch, or turned on the water. Everything in the apartment was still, including its occupants. Ambiance we might have once considered peaceful carried us toward our demise.

My consciousness faded. I heard and saw and thought nothing. For days? Maybe. Hours on hours, certainly. Life vanished.

Until I heard a loud BANG!

The insides of my heavy eyelids turned from black to burnt orange. The red door. It was open. When my eyes managed to peel halfway back for the briefest of moments, I saw light pushing through the entryway. Behind the glow I made out the silhouettes of Cee-Cee and her mother in a small crowd of people. Their long, flowy black hair made them easy to identify.

Paramedics and police couldn't have known what they were witnessing until they got closer. Then they sprang into action.

Hands hoisted and gently stretched my frail frame along what felt like a bed. It rolled loudly against the floor. A cool breeze whisking over my face told me we'd crossed the threshold. I heard inaudible voices in the distance. Then, nothing, again.

A long sidewalk coiled from our apartment complex to the street. I imagine myself being wheeled down this sidewalk as concerned neighbors lined each side, hands covering their mouths, tears moistening their cheeks. Perhaps some of them said a prayer for me, kissed my forehead or caressed my unresponsive hand. How I might've liked to have shown gratitude for such compassion.

I remembered too much, but also forgot a lot. I forgot how my mother and I were before our love was interrupted by tragedy. I forgot she'd always taken care of us until one day she didn't and even on that day, convinced our floor was contaminated to the point of untouchable, she lowered to her hands and knees and crawled with us on her back. She touched the poisoned wood so her children wouldn't have to.

Memories of "Mommy" slid a little further outside my mind every night. I forgot there were things I didn't know. That broken fathers are broken men, broken husbands, broken partners. It wasn't only me who suffered at their hands. We all sat deteriorating alone in our apartment, enduring the results of my mother's maltreatment. Perhaps she suffered most of all. Because to me, Daddy was perfect, and she didn't ever speak ill of him, not even to defend the image I held of her.

Grandma brought us back to Gary after we were released from the hospital a few days later. Danny and I left first. We played our way through the halls as staff smiled, waved, and wished us well. Our mother had to stay a little while longer. She'd had a "nervous breakdown," Grandma said.

We left Daddy behind, along with the girl I was when with him. I forgot the illusion of safety found in a strong embrace.

I didn't remember the tender love of a man sworn to protect me. I lost the bright moments and the promises kept and the blameless bliss of feeling like someone's daughter. Everything Daddy ever gave me, erased. Then, although he came home to Gary for visits sometimes, I erased him, too.

Passed along to the next man I would know as my father, I cleared my heart's canvas to allow him space for the creation of new magic. All he put there was more emptiness and unsatisfied longing, a father void large enough to hold my mother wound. I climbed into it when he left me waiting in front of that window and forgot I wasn't always so sad.

3

Set Me Loose

Grandma called my name and nudged my shoulders until my eyes unsealed. Then she vanished into the kitchen to continue making breakfast. She'd instilled enough obedience in me to know she didn't have to stand there and make sure I got up to prepare myself for school.

I rolled out of the living room sofa bed and tugged at my pink nightgown. Making my way down the dim hallway, I ran my hand against the bumpy wall to aid my bearings. Mornings are gray in the Midwest. Rarely was there early sunlight with which to align your awakening spirit.

The bathroom was small. Grandma kept it nice though, with laced towels we weren't allowed to touch and satin curtains covering a tiny window above the bathtub. She didn't only make do with what she had, but made the best of it.

When you came into her home, you saw plastic covering the living room furniture and a strategic placement of doilies on the coffee table. In the dining room stood one of her most prized possessions, a China cabinet filled with geisha dolls and fancy dinnerware. Grandma appreciated her possessions and if the items or surroundings were not elegant, she would make them so. Her modest bathroom was no different.

The blue toilet was immediately inside the entryway, then the sink, then the tub. Boom-boom-boom. There was no room to do much other than what you'd come in to do. I turned toward the wall and stood on my tiptoes to flick the light switch up once my feet hit the cold tile, and shut the door behind me. Grandma made us take baths at night, so, my morning routine was low maintenance. I had to move fast to allow Danny, my aunt, and other people in the house to complete their own daybreak rituals.

Like every other morning, I went through a practice of using the restroom then washing my face. Next, I brushed my teeth over the toilet because the sink was too high for us kids to spit into. Mid-brush, my strokes slowed, slower and slower with each back-and-forth motion.

Oh no. It's happening again.

The sadness enveloped me. I could track its gradual rise within my body. I could sense it washing over, consuming me, little by little, then entirely. I tried to keep going. I moved the toothbrush side to side, up and down over a couple of teeth while water collected beneath my pupils before rolling down my face.

Sometimes it happened while I was playing outside, or in bed awaiting sleep. It happened whether I was alone or surrounded by people. This time, it happened while I hunched over the toilet brushing my teeth, before the day could give me reason to grieve.

I had to hurry though. I didn't want to be yelled at or whooped for taking too long. If in the bathroom longer than Grandma expected me to be, my food would get cold, and she'd have to rush us to school. I knew the stakes and the consequences of my dallying.

Danny and I stayed with Grandma while our mother attended college, worked nights at a gas station, and strived to put the pieces of her life back together. As far as we could tell, there were no lingering detrimental effects from her mental break. Still, her life was upended. She returned to Gary with no husband, no home, no money, loads of guilt, and little confidence in her parenting ability. Help remained necessary. Her mother stepped in and stepped up.

Grandma assumed the responsibility of raising us, but after rearing the ten children she'd birthed, her patience was paper thin. Danny and I were lucky if she told us even one time to do something we already knew we should do, and she didn't ever repeat her demands. The reminder was her five-foot frame bursting into the bathroom and flipping the toilet's lid down, so she could sit and bend me over her knee. Or her storming outside to whoop Danny in front of our friends after he let the ball we were tossing around go astray and hit the house.

Spare the rod, spoil the child was Grandma's motto. She derived it from her religious teachings and charged herself with utilizing the method to keep us well behaved. She made me and Danny stay in line so we didn't have to get in line. Whoopings weren't used as a last resort, but as Grandma's first option. To her, prompt physical discipline was love, protection, and lesson all rolled into one.

I had to hurry. *Keep going*, I told myself. *Move fast.* But my sobbing went from silent to violent in an instant. I couldn't get it to stop. I never could once it started. Each attempt reminded me of my powerlessness. My only option was to wait until the fit was done with me.

I wailed and trembled, terrified by the loss of control over my own body. While jabbing a toothbrush around inside my mouth, toothpaste spilled into the toilet. Followed by the contents of my stomach. The force dropped me to my knees. My belly kept falling into itself, trying to push more up, but nothing came.

Grandma shoved her way into the bathroom, slipping through an open sliver of the door I'd curled up behind. She looked down to the floor at me squeezing my shaking legs against my chest. "What's wrong?" she asked.

"I don't know," I gave the same answer whenever my ordinary moments turned tragic. "I just feel sad."

They all wanted answers. Watching cartoons once with Danny, he turned to laugh with me at something I should've found funny. But my head was down as I tried to stifle sniffles. "What's wrong with you?" He kept asking, over and over, looking part curious, part annoyed until I shrugged my shoulders. Over it, he turned back toward the television.

Standing before the church congregation when Grandma marched me up for prayer, the pastor asked, "Why are you unhappy?" I searched for a response that might satisfy him before admitting I had none. He looked worried, staring at me with furrowed eyebrows, then dipping his finger into a jar of oil and painting a cross on my forehead before resting his palm on top of it. Everyone shouted in the background as he commanded the devil to set me loose. "In the name of Jesus!" The congregation stretched their hands toward me, praying along with the pastor. Grandma stood next to me, waving her arms in the air. When the spectacle ended, I returned to my seat, none the happier.

Dr. Harris, whose kindergarten class I joined at Locke Elementary in the middle of the school year, was an older lady with a shoulder-length mushroom haircut. She wore pearl earrings, white lace dresses, and carried herself with stout grace. You could tell she had money. During class, Dr. Harris would hold my chin, lift my face toward hers and say my eyes were "too pretty to always look so sad." She wanted to know why I always looked on the verge of tears.

I had Dr. Harris again for first grade. There too, she inquired. When I was no longer her student, she passed me in the halls and stopped to pay me special attention. She tilted her head to one side and smiled a little, the way you do when the smile is filled with more sympathy than joy. "How are you, Acamea?"

"Fine," I always answered.

She returned an affirmative nod but her face displayed disbelief.

My family got close to Dr. Harris. She was also a prophet, considered a powerful minister in the region. It was the same thing when we attended one of her services. She'd spot me in the audience, walk over holding a microphone, and greet me in a sing-songy voice.

"Ohhh and when I look upon this child who was in my kindergarten claaaasssss... How are you tonight, Acameaaaaaa?"

She pointed the microphone my direction.

"Fine." I said in the tiniest, squeakiest voice.

Everyone in the crowd gave me the head tilt and half-smile.

Crying spells didn't happen at school, though I felt just as sad. Only at home or Grandma's house. Among my peers, I wielded some restraint. I might've looked like I would cry but somehow didn't. I think I was afraid of the inevitable teasing. No kid wants to melt down in front of their friends, and we were in an innocent stretch of life. When you're a small child, everyone is your friend. School also offered countless distractions. With teachers talking, kids playing, naps, lunch, library, and recess, there wasn't much opportunity for me to sit with my sorrow until it spilled out of me.

I could escape myself when we ran out onto the playground for recess. Defying gravity, I swung to deliverance. I'd ask my schoolmates to push me harder, higher, to the point where chains connecting the swing to its frame were almost parallel to the ground. At the height of my ascent, I'd jump off, sometimes falling, scraping my hands and knees on the gravel-covered ground. It wouldn't hurt until later, when I was back at my desk and the adrenaline wore off and I realized I'd done it for a short while—set myself free.

Despondence became my default. I couldn't explain it. Couldn't find the words to describe how my heart broke a little every day. Every. Single. Day. It broke despite not ever starting from whole. Until the ever-present, compounding brokenness eventually broke me.

Grandma didn't yell at me for taking too long in the bathroom this time. She lifted me to my feet, unfurled my nightgown, and wiped the white streaks from my face. One of her arms flushed the toilet while the other wrapped around my waist and held me upright. She rinsed my toothbrush and placed it back into a cup on the sink. "Go eat breakfast," she instructed.

I dragged my heaviness back down the hallway and into the kitchen. It was often filled with the early aroma of smothered potatoes. Exerting my last bit of strength, I climbed up to the bench framing the wooden table and glared at the plate of food prepared for me.

Attempting to muster an appetite, I sat there unable to imagine putting any food inside the stomach that had just betrayed me and remained sorely unsettled. But we also got in trouble for being wasteful. "There are starving children in Africa," Grandma always reminded me and Danny.

I sat at this table for hours sometimes. I'd fallen asleep here and awoken to see a plate still in front of me, waiting for me to eat it clean. Grandma was more lenient and gentler than usual today, but I didn't want to push it. I placed my hands together in front of my face to say grace.

"God is great. God is good. Lord, we thank you for our food."

My mouth tasted like paste. Yet, I picked up my fork and took tiny bites of breakfast, suppressing a gag reflex with each forced swallow. I am too young to feel this old. To be this tired. Lord, can I be anyone but myself? With all the hope that last time was the last time drained from my body, I sometimes followed with another prayer, a silent prayer to make me think I still had a chance at being someone different.

"Fix me."

Amen.

My mother cried a lot during her pregnancy at eighteen years old. She cried when she thought about disappointing her parents. She cried when her ex-boyfriend denied being my father. She cried when he drove past the house with his new girlfriend in the car and stopped to wave at her—serving up his utter disregard with a side of psychological torture. She believed she must've passed her incessant sorrow through the womb and down to me. It was, to her, the only explanation for a child who knew nothing of depression to be clutched in its grasp. Not leftover trauma from California. Not being stripped away from Daddy. She thought the sadness was inadvertently her fault, a generational curse.

My mother birthing me at eighteen meant she was twenty-three when San Diego happened. Twenty-three. How could she handle such mature devastation? I ask myself this now, only in full adulthood having comprehended how young she was when it all went down. Because no matter the age of our parents, we tend to only see them as just that—parents. I never imagined my mother as a girl or envisioned her without the capacity to understand what was happening to her and the language to explain how it felt. I only saw that both my fathers were gone, literally, and my mother, figuratively. She was around in the physical sense but not present, barely speaking or interacting with me.

I didn't make interaction easy. Her intermittent tries were met with silence or the avoidance of eye contact until she grew hesitant to try at all. I didn't understand that my mother was still in her youth. *How come no one loves me?* was all I wanted to know. And I commenced laying bricks that would build my house of resentment toward those who made me ask.

I didn't have enough information to resent Champ's mother, but when she asked to see me, I was every bit of indifferent. My first visit, I entered her apartment building and wrinkled my nose at the stench of food. An odd odor filled the hallways and stairwell as we climbed to her third-floor unit. It got stronger and stronger until I reached its source, her kitchen. Infinitely sweet and utterly polite, I resisted saying anything. Every time I came over it smelled the same. Nothing I knew of could possibly give off such a scent and remain edible.

Sometimes I showed up to new shoes or a dress. I'd try on the clothes and model in the living room while she chuckled, "Look at Grandmama's baby." I twirled and smiled and performed, fueled by the praise. She seemed ecstatic to have me as her grandchild. My presence hadn't ever brought anyone such obvious joy. Grandmama bounced around the apartment like she was entertaining a superstar, asking if I wanted anything, digging up mementos to show me, handling me as though I might break if she spoke too loudly or hugged me too tightly.

I think, aside from intermittent Champ visits, I was the only guest she had. It was as though she saved up all her personal news in the between time and ran it all down to me. "They changed Grandmama's shift at work. I had to get a new tire put on the car. Grandmama hurt her back." All her ordinary moments tumbled out like a grocery list. I sat and listened, sensing it was all she wanted, someone with whom to share pieces of herself. The recounting was always succinct, fifteen minutes tops, before she shifted the conversation to asking about me.

A nurse who did well for herself financially, Grandmama tried to fill the gaps her son left in my life. Gifts were common. In addition to clothes and shoes, I got baby dolls, books, stuffed animals, Barbies, and anything else she thought an early-grade schoolgirl would like. We went for rides in her fancy gold Mercury Cougar with its tan leather seats. She drove us all kinds of places. To stores where I could pick out my own gifts, to the hospital where she could introduce me to her co-workers, to her beautician who did my hair.

With Grandmama, I got my first Jheri Curl. It took forever to install. The lady had to apply the creamy product, wrap small sections of my hair around plastic curling rods, sit me under a hair dryer, unspool all the rods, and polish off the finished product with liquid activator.

Ignore that when I wore my curl to school along with a red leather vest, older students called me Michael Jackson. Forget how the activator and styling gel ruined my pillows with head-sized grease spots resistant to detergent. I LOVED it! Loved how it bounced when freshly done. How sleek, shiny, and soft it was. I felt like a grownup since most of the adults I saw in the 80s had Jheri Curls. My mother, uncles, aunts, and parents of the cool kids all rocked the hairstyle. Most of my friends weren't allowed to get one. Their moms said the chemicals were too harsh. Yet, here I was, participating in the trend. One of the unusual times I had something others coveted. I sported the Jheri Curl in my kindergarten graduation photo.

There were knickknacks and framed photographs all over Grandmama's apartment. Sports trophies covered a shelf near the television. I never asked about him, but each visit Grandmama mentioned Champ, her only child, and his trophies. Compelled to sing his praises, her eyes glossed above an ear-to-ear grin while she held gold or silver mini-statues and delivered a nostalgic Champ history lesson. Most trophies depicted a guy holding a football or basketball. A bunch of medals dangled from ribbons. Awards adorned the living room, remnants of a past life, the climactic chapter of a larger story.

Champ was a burly six-foot-four, well-equipped to become a gifted athlete. When I met him he had a thick mustache and close-shaven beard. But back then, in Grandmama's photos, he had a smooth beige face and a wide smile accentuated by dimples. Combine his physical stature with his jock status and easiness on the eyes, and it wasn't hard to see what my mother and other women saw in him.

The kind of guy who had a heart encasing the word "mom" tattooed across his shoulder, I suspect Champ's exterior fooled many. One might think a mama's boy was caring and sensitive. Perhaps he was, just not with me. Or with his high school girlfriend. Nonetheless, mama defended her boy. Rather than lament his wrongs she tried to make them right.

"Champ has been really busy," Grandmama led into after gushing over an award or Polaroid. "Champ loves you. If you ever need anything and can't get ahold of him, you let Grandmama know." She made me promise. I broke it.

Maybe Grandmama was protecting me from a reality harsher than what I'd already experienced. What else was she supposed to say? Your father just wanted to have sex with your mother and didn't want a kid? She tried to make me feel loved, and valuable. She wanted me to believe Champ's absence wasn't my fault, or his.

I don't recall Grandmama referring to her son as my father. She never said, "your dad." It was always "Champ." Maybe some part of her did know he hadn't earned the title and wasn't comfortable using it.

A few years into our sporadic get-togethers, Grandmama re-
tired from nursing as her aging body developed its own health
problems. Effects apparent to me began with her using a cane,
the type with three rubber-tipped prongs on the end for added
stability. It was a chore for her to get down the stairs to let me
into the building. She labored back up to her apartment, placing
both feet on one step at a time.

When we arrived, Grandmama let out a deep sigh and
propped her leg up on the couch. Soon she stopped coming
down altogether, simply buzzing me in when I pressed the button to call her apartment.

With Grandmama unable to get around well anymore, my
visits became subdued. There was less vigor in her conversation, as though summoning the strength to speak was too much.
Her cheerful greetings were replaced with a low, raspy drawl of
"Howwww's Grandmama's baby?" She smiled less and had the
face of a person in persistent pain, wincing with every slight
movement. She held her breath and bit her lip for the big movements, like rising from the sofa. Instead of asking if I wanted
anything to eat, she encouraged me to go into the kitchen and
help myself to whatever I found.

The atmosphere was still soaked with the smell of ques-
tionable cuisine. Rummaging through the kitchen, I stood on
my tiptoes and quietly lifted the lids of pots simmering on the
stove, wrinkling my nose in the steam that escaped. Inside I
found ham hocks, black eyed peas, neck bones, lima beans,
chitterlings, and stuff I couldn't name. It was satisfying to connect certain foods with odors, to know what I didn't want to eat,
ever. Chitterlings.

After conducting my investigations, I made my way to the
snack cakes and potato chips Grandmama stashed in the cup-
board specifically for my stay. I could eat as much as I wanted,
whenever I wanted. The snacks helped occupy me as I sat on the

floor watching cartoons. Grandmama whispered from the couch every hour or so, "You alright baby?"

Sometimes I stared up, studying the shelf of trophies and display of photographs, inventing stories about Champ in my head. Things like, *maybe he looked happy because it was a day his team won their basketball game.* Or, *maybe my mother took the photo of him in front of his car.*

I considered whether Champ might come check on his sick mother. Where was he? I looked toward Grandmama's apartment door whenever I heard footsteps, waiting to hear the jingle of keys or watch the doorknob twist. Is it him? I thought I might trick him into seeing me until footsteps dissolved in the distance.

In short order, visits with Grandmama ceased entirely. I didn't think much of it. I'd learned to exist in the present, to not get my hopes up nor think about things before or after they happened. Visiting Grandmama was fine, but not something I looked forward to. Sitting with her forced me to remember my father. I was surrounded by literal reminders that he was an actual person, one who chose not to show up for me. The photos and trophies and narratives reminded me there was a reality that included Champ. He went from buried in my subconscious to almost real again. I went to being disappointed again, confused, again.

Going to Grandmama's apartment was like being introduced to a stranger who lived in the life of the stranger who was supposed to mean something to me. Over, and over. I didn't see her enough to grow comfortable in the environment. She referred to me as her grandbaby, but the puzzle piece between us was missing, and I couldn't ignore the space where it should have been. I wasn't upset when the visits stopped. To me, what came to an end was having my father's blatant absence shoved in my face every few weeks.

Still, Grandmama called sometimes to promise our meetings would resume once she recovered. I pretended to be excited. Then the phone calls stopped too.

As if on cue, while Grandmama faded away, her estranged husband entered the picture. Champ's dad walked up and down Grandma's block more times on more days than I was aware, trying to catch me playing outside. Sometimes he succeeded.

Danny and I both had bikes but couldn't ride further than two houses in either direction. So, we'd go two houses down, turn around in the neighbor's driveway, and go two houses down the other way. It was fun enough for two sheltered little kids who didn't get to do much of anything.

We popped wheelies over small bumps in the sidewalk to add to the excitement. This was easier for my brother on his BMX than it was for me. I had a cruiser with a pink banana seat and a basket hanging from the front. My wheelies could barely be called such, but I didn't care. I loved my bike and riding it was one of my favorite things.

I turned around in a neighbor's driveway to head back toward the house one day. Looking ahead at Danny who was always faster and thus in front of me, I was giggling and talking instead of paying attention to my surroundings. Once I noticed the figure stumbling up alongside me, it was too late.

Champ's dad was about three feet away and getting closer. I could smell what I didn't know at the time was cheap alcohol. "My graaaandbaaaby," he managed to drawl while stretching out his arms and puckering his wet lips. "Come give grandpa a kiss."

I leaped off my bike while it was still rolling and let it fall to the ground as I ran screaming to Grandma's house. She kept the inside door open to watch us, but the screen door stayed locked to prevent us from running in and out—letting in flies and somehow also running up her light bill.

I was wailing and banging on the screen door, looking over my shoulder as though trying to elude a monster. It felt like that's what was happening. I hadn't seen a drunk person before. He trudged down the sidewalk like any zombie I'd ever seen in movies. The all-around bizarreness of this peculiar figure attempting to put his hands and mouth on me in real life was horrifying.

Champ's dad knew not to push his luck past the lawn. He stood well-groomed and overdressed at its edge, his hair slicked back like Billy Dee Williams. He had a neatly trimmed mustache to boot. You could tell he must've been some kind of heartthrob in his day. Perhaps he still was. Perhaps it's why he always wore a three-piece suit, wingtip shoes, and sometimes a trench coat with a fedora hat. Whether it be a bar or a woman's house, he was clearly leaving or heading somewhere warranting such apparel.

Drunk Billy Dee stood leering at me from the other side of the grass, saying "Come onnn," with his arms still outstretched. His gold tooth glistening in the sunshine. Finally, Grandma came and let me into the house. She begged of me, "What? What's going on?" before glancing outside.

We both watched Champ's dad through the screen door until he chuckled, waved his hand in a dismissive gesture, and resumed shuffling down the block. I waited a little while to make sure he was gone before venturing back outside. "Why are you scared of him?" Danny asked. He wasn't. He always stood smiling, alternating between observing my utter unraveling and the man causing it. I didn't have a definitive answer. I didn't know why I was so afraid while my younger brother straddled his bike, unfazed.

Here was a random man barely able to stay upright, puckering his moist, stinking lips in my face and trying to wrap his arms around me. I thought something must've been wrong with him, especially since I didn't know who he was that first time.

The instant trauma didn't subside when Grandma explained our relation. "He's your other grandfather," she said. "Like how Mrs. Wilson is your other grandmother." Grandma called him "a mess."

This supposed grandfather probably caught me outside a handful of times before he stopped coming around. It was always the same disgraceful display. How different things might have gone had he thought to find me just once while sober. I might have asked him about Champ.

4

Rust Belt

Gary is the birthplace of the Jacksons. For the less talented, less fortunate citizens, the city is one where needs far surpass opportunities for fulfillment. It is itself a source of sadness for those searching or susceptible. My mother didn't do anything to find herself navigating unfortunate circumstances except be one of six sons and four daughters born to her parents in a city that quickly lost its promise, and then fall in love with a product of that same environment.

In its day, Gary was an industrial town where any man willing to get his hands dirty could make good money. My grandparents left Brinkley, Arkansas and settled here, chasing a better life. They bought a tiny mustard-colored four-bedroom house and filled it with an abundance of children. Three small bedrooms were positioned right next to each other in an L-shaped pattern, with the den converted to a fourth. Everyone shared rooms in the 950 square-foot, one-level home. Some shared beds.

Positioned about thirty miles east of Chicago, Illinois, Gary sits on the southern border of Lake Michigan. This made the city ripe for the development of a booming steel mill industry that Grandaddy was able to get into at its most fruitful. I didn't see him much. He'd rise before the sun, get fully dressed, make a cup of coffee, and read his morning paper at the dining room table before leaving for the day.

Sometimes when Grandaddy ventured to the front of the house, Danny and I happened to be in the living room watching *ThunderCats* or *The Smurfs*, depending on who woke and turned on the television first. We liked most of the same shows. But my brother also liked the action cartoons most other boys his age enjoyed. *ThunderCats*, *He-Man*, and *Dragon Ball* were of no interest to me. "Turn to something else," I'd whine if he beat me to the punch and put on one of these shows. He often did as I requested unless he was already too invested in the plot to miss the ending.

If I didn't wake to catch a morning glimpse, I wouldn't see Grandaddy until he returned in the evening, and only for the minutes it took to exchange pleasantries with the household and head back into his bedroom.

After long, hard days he came home exhausted, in search of only peace. Peace is hard to come by in a tiny over-occupied house. Grandaddy spent the few remaining evening hours in his room with the door shut. When dinner was ready, Grandma made his plate, filled his favorite oversized mug with root beer, sat it all on a copper tray, and carried it to him.

Most days, Grandaddy wore different variations of the same outfit, slacks and a flannel or button-down shirt of some sort. The only deviation came during church. He was a deacon who guarded the doors to the sanctuary wearing white gloves and a crisp black suit.

Hands clasped firmly across his torso, a smirk emerged from Grandaddy's stone face when saints caught the holy ghost and ran shouting through the aisles. Not once had he lost such control of himself. His signature smirk was about the extent of his expressions and the only indication he was ever amused.

When someone got carried away, if a woman threw her body around and looked like she might hurt herself or pass out from the exertion, Grandaddy would walk over and extend his arms behind her. "Calm down, calm down," he'd say in a low, soothing tone. Sometimes the woman shook her head and sat down, the way you do when overwhelmed. Other times, she fell into complete submission, knowing Grandaddy was there to ensure a gentle landing.

The show could go on for fifteen minutes, easy. If the organist and the drummer got going, their dueling melodies would rile up the entire congregation. Everyone would be shouting, dancing, running, or—at the very least—waving their arms in the air. Grandaddy made his way to each of those most overcome by the moment and either held them up or laid them down as the situation required. Once the commotion tapered off, he returned to his post at the sanctuary's entryway, crossed his hands and resumed an unflappable demeanor.

Grandaddy was a husband who took care of his wife and financially supported their household. Bills were always paid, and Grandma got the newest, hottest items she wanted. She had one of the first gigantic microwaves. She had an early floor-model television, which was basically a massive tube TV mounted atop a swiveling base. She was also one of the first people on the block with a VCR. They didn't have fancy cars or a big house, but my grandparents did well, especially by hood standards.

While my mother was in high school, she watched Gary go the way of other Rust Belt cities. Plants shut down. Businesses left. Well-to-do families abandoned their homes while my grandparents stayed. Aside from the lucky ones like Grandaddy, who were able to hold on to a spot in the steel mills, the decimated economy left mostly desperate people motivated to take desperate measures. In came the violence and the drugs, and the city receiving its title as our nation's murder capital. Out went the hope.

Here is where my mother graduated into the real world and had a daughter whose father refused to claim her. Then she had a son with her husband, got out of town, but was forced to return, fleeing an abusive marriage that almost killed us all. She might've chosen better with better choices. She might've given more with more left to give.

The decline my mother witnessed while in high school only intensified when we came back to Gary. My grandparents did okay financially, but alone, we were poor. And I knew we were poor because my friends at school told me. It was an accident though. They thought I already knew.

Standing before a room full of people remains a most vulnerable experience, no matter the people or the room. All eyes and judgments are on you. But I didn't feel this way until sharpening my pencil at the front of the class one fifth-grade morning.

The pencil sharpener was for more than sharpening pencils; it's where kids went to show off a new outfit or shoes. It gave you a couple minutes to flex in the spotlight. Everyone couldn't help but see you.

The cutest boy in the class, Wesley Williams, would stroll to the front, slide his pencil into the sharpener, and do one hundred other things before sharpening. He'd pull a brush from his back pocket and smooth it over his deep waves, turning toward the class and licking his lips in the process. Once done with the display, he sometimes bent down to brush nonexistent dirt from his Reebok Pumps. Other times, he tugged at the basketball jersey or Starter pullover jacket he was wearing as if it were not already creased perfectly against his body. He'd press buttons on his Casio watch, joke with other students, and do anything else he could think of until finally completing the task at hand and returning to his seat.

"You like me, Acamea?" Wesley said once while going through his usual front-of-the-class theatrics.

Huh? I looked up from my desk. Is he joking? Wesley mimicked a kissing motion in my direction and repeated the question.

"You like me, don't you?"

I wasn't sure what to say. It felt like a setup. I wasn't one of the popular girls he was into. I looked around the classroom. Every head was turned toward me, awaiting a response.

I shrugged. "I don't know. I guess."

Not only was Wesley cute and well-dressed, but he was also on the basketball team. A trifecta of attractive attributes. Everyone liked him and he knew it. "I like you too baby," he said, cutting his eyes toward a teammate and sneering hard enough to reveal his dimple.

"Weird," I thought, and went back to my schoolwork.

I had no ulterior motives when making visits to the pencil sharpener. I wasn't trying to be seen. Only looking to prepare for class.

At school I kept busy in my own world. Studying for spelling bees. Reading my textbooks. School followed a familiar formula: be perfect, do as asked, be rewarded. Your family showers you with praise and displays your accomplishments on the refrigerator. Your mother brags about you to her friends. Everyone claps for you. I was good at school like I was good at church.

A year earlier, in fourth grade, I had a goal to win the school spelling bee. I stayed up studying my list of words every night leading up to it. One word stuck out to me. Whoever typed up the list had spelled *geese* as *gease*. I knew it was wrong. Well, I thought I knew it was wrong but how could it be when adults were always right? That's what I'd been taught. I examined and recited from the list as given and hoped I didn't get that word when the time came.

The time came.

The cafeteria was converted to an auditorium and stuffed with people. The entire school was there, every teacher, student, and staff worker. My family was there, Grandma, my mother, and of course Danny, who was a third grader at Locke. Perched at the front of the stage, I stared through the open doors at the back of the room and out into an empty hallway instead of at the crowd. I visualized each word in my head before spelling it out loud. Contestants were knocked out every round before my turn came again.

Soon, there was just me and one other girl left. We went back and forth, toe to toe, and then it happened. "Acamea, your word is *geese*." I froze. I knew what my list of words said but I also knew it was wrong. Would they judge me on what was correct or what they'd assigned me? I weighed the question while the moderator smiled. Such a simple word. I'm sure she thought this would be a no-brainer after the complex vocabulary I'd gotten through without hesitation. I considered the best course of action as my time dwindled away. Finally, I opened my mouth.

"Geese. G-E . . . A-S-E, geese." The moderator, who also happened to be my teacher, frowned. "I'm sorry, Acamea. That's incorrect." The other girl jumped and clapped for herself as she was announced the winner. Her family rose to their feet and cheered. I looked over at mine, at Grandma's look of disappointment, certain I was cheated out of the win.

After the spelling bee I showed my teacher the list of words given to me. Her mouth dropped when she saw *gease*. She lifted the eyeglasses hanging from a chain around her neck, slid them onto her nose to get a better look, and scurried out of the classroom to show the other teachers who'd organized the spelling bee. A few minutes later she came back and apologized. There was nothing they could do now. "Why didn't you say something sooner, Acamea?" The answer was I didn't trust myself as much as I trusted the rules and the precedent of not questioning grown-ups. But I didn't have those words yet. I just shrugged.

I showed Grandma the spelling list too. She was livid and I was redeemed. It wasn't my fault.

Now in fifth grade, I was determined to win every prize, earn every award, receive every recognition. I was committed to doing what I was good at, achieving. And I was learning of more opportunities to make myself somebody.

Too oblivious to know I should be self-conscious, I bounced around classrooms more carefree than my social currency could afford. I joined the student council and raved about things I got to do as a member. "We're going on a field trip to the mayor's office." Or "I'm learning Russian during the summer."

"So?" a classmate responded once. Normally, no one paid me much attention. They gave me *why are you telling us?* looks when I spoke about things that excited me. Ebony's verbal acknowledgment was startling. "I'm just saying," I mumbled. "Don't nobody care about the student council," she said and waved her hand before turning back to talk with her friends.

I raved about my academic privileges until I started getting flippant looks and realized that kids who deemed such programs lame were annoyed by what they considered bragging. Grandma told me they were just jealous, but it was hard to believe. There was nothing about me I found worth their envy.

School was another avenue for me to garner acknowledgment. It didn't bring me joy but served as a place where I could escape sadness. The other kids came here to have fun with their friends, wear their new outfits, and go to basketball games. I didn't know what their mothers and fathers and grandmothers were like, but they seemed far less concerned with proving themselves to anyone. I would have much rather been in their place than mine. The kids weren't jealous. They were appalled at my audacity to not be invisible.

Whether it was much of a factor or not, the irritation of my classmates had been building by the fateful morning I bounced my braided pigtails to the pencil sharpener. One of them mentioned Concord Village, a well-known local housing community. Then someone else said, "That's where Acamea lives." I whipped my head around toward the room, smiled, and confirmed the declaration with a goofy nod. "Those are the projects," Ebony chimed in with the same disgust held when she'd said, "So?" in response to my rambling about school activities.

I stopped sharpening and looked at the matter-of-fact expression on her face, her raised eyebrows and cold gaze. She was tall with a mahogany complexion and long black hair pressed to perfection. She was gorgeous, even when she was ugly. The cute guy next to her, Wesley, flashed a smug smile. The girl next to him squinted as though confused.

She was saying I lived in the ghetto. Was she saying that I was ghetto? That I was one of the kids they snickered at and called broke? No one told me there was anything different about the townhome we moved into after leaving our little yellow and white house.

"I don't live in the projects!" roared out of my mouth. But I did. They knew it. Standing there in hand-me-down blue jeans and off-brand sneakers, I should have known it too. I should have known I was poor. I think my not knowing kind of saddened the other students. Their faces changed. I'd seen these looks before, the tilted heads, the drooping mouths, the prolonged glances at one another. It was pity. No one challenged my response.

The teacher, Mr. Gilbert, looked up from his desk but also said nothing. He turned his balding head toward me and watched. Everyone watched me watching them. The room fell so silent I could hear the throbbing of my heart. It rose from my chest to my throat. I wanted to run and hide because it felt like tears were imminent.

Mercy.

The lump surrendered beneath my swallows long enough for me to finish sharpening my pencil. A slow grinding sound echoed through the stagnant air. I could feel the stares of students piercing my back like lasers.

If I could have stayed there until class ended to avoid turning this wrecked version of myself toward those faces, I would have. Unfortunately, class hadn't yet started. I clutched my over-sharpened writing tool and returned to my seat in the back of the room, rolling my watering eyes at classmates along the way for daring to speak such nonsense.

From then on, the gloves came off. Refusing to allow my continued obliviousness, classmates pointed out when the label on my shoes read "Air," not followed by "Jordan." But I'd chosen the pair myself, with pleasure, from the aisles of Payless. The kids let me know when I was wearing a past season's clothing. They said things like, "I had your shirt two years ago," and laughed. My few brand-name items were also unacceptable. I quickly discovered nothing I had was up to par so neither could I be. Didn't matter if it was new. Didn't matter if it was designer. There were levels to fashion and style that I could not reach.

Though they resided poverty-adjacent, cooler kids wanted me in my poverty-stricken place. The distance was wide enough to draw a line between us. I stayed on my side.

I did what I'd long ago learned to do in hurtful conditions, closed my mouth. I stood at the very back of lines when we walked the halls. I waited to sharpen my pencil until it was an absolute necessity and did it fast, covering one of my feet with the other and rushing back to my desk once done. I did what they wanted, made myself invisible. Not only to avoid ridicule but because, well, how dare I show myself as though I deserved anyone's attention?

I sat with my head down on my desk more often, but turned to one side so I could see what was happening. Inevitably, Mr. Gilbert called me to solve a math problem at the chalkboard. I responded with a muffled, "No."

"What did you say?" he asked.

"No."

"I'm not asking," he said. "Get up here and solve the problem."

I unfolded one arm from beneath my head, raised it into the air, and stuck my middle finger up. My classmates gasped. Some laughed. Mr. Gilbert was beside himself.

"G-G-Get outside!" He could barely spit the words out, he was so livid. "Now!" A red-faced Mr. Gilbert pointed out into the hallway.

I got up, slogged out into the hall, and assumed my position facing the wall. I'd never been paddled but saw other kids stand with their hands against the painted brick with feet shoulder width apart. Mr. Gilbert was right behind me, holding his flat, wooden paddle. It was thick and smooth. Like a narrow cutting board covered in little screw-sized holes. He gave me a swat. It stung like a mother, but I didn't react. I was angry, too, furious that he would do that to me, call me to the front of the class after he'd seen what had happened. After he'd witnessed me trying to stay hidden.

He gave me another swat. Still nothing. Mr. Gilbert took a step back. His face softened. "Go to your seat."

Back inside the classroom, I again rested my head on the desk. Face down, I shook with tears in front of my classmates for the first time I can remember.

Unraveling the pencil sharpener exchange, I knew those kids were right. It explained everything, including why our home was burglarized several times a year. I wasn't yet at a point where

I understood wages and cost of living. If I were, I would've known a single mother attending college while working nights as a gas station clerk couldn't afford a two-story, three-bedroom, two-bathroom home under ordinary circumstances. In an instant, a life considered adequate felt like one of which I should be ashamed.

I lied about having new things. I'd polish Danny's old sneakers and wear them to school as my latest. My mother thought it more important for a boy to have nice athletic shoes. They were visibly worn with wrinkled toe boxes and blackened soles. The sneakers were also at least a couple sizes too big for me.

My two best friends, Candace and Keonna, were kind enough to play along when inspecting my "new" kicks. They usually just gave me a slow head nod, except once, when I came to school in a pair of hi-top white Nikes with a red swoosh Danny had run into the ground and tossed aside. I had to tie the Nikes extra tight around my ankles to hold them on my feet. They looked like clown shoes. Unfurled clown shoes slathered in white shoe polish. The best it could do was turn the cracked, dirty leather a faint gray.

Candace looked down as I approached her and Keonna in the hallway. I offered a preemptive explanation. "Danny messed them up! I let him wear the shoes over the weekend."

"Dang, what did he do?" Candace asked. "Bite them?"

We laughed. I didn't dare wear the red-and-white hi-top Nikes again, and my two best friends continued to avoid explicitly calling me out on the recurring foolishness. They were kind and seemed entirely unconcerned with my appearance. Yet, in the unspectacular heat of a moment, I punched one of them in the stomach for saying something I didn't like.

I punched Keonna, the one who wore gold chains and leather jackets while the kids who always said things I didn't like egged me on. I punched her because I couldn't punch them. Because we have a terrible tendency to punish those closest to us for the pain caused by those ostensibly out of reach.

Keonna could've run with the popular crowd. She had the look and the status. But she and I gravitated toward one another, along with the third member of our clique, because we were always several inches shorter than everyone else in our grade. We were the smallest kids in our classes. Everyone referred to me, Candace and Keonna as "Li'l Bit." It seemed natural to hang out together. From there we developed a genuine bond, but it started with simple shared experience.

After the punch, Keonna and I reconciled without ever speaking of the incident. I understood. To preserve her image, she had to ensure she wasn't too closely associated with someone like me. Understanding was mutual. I think Keonna comprehended how my embarrassment might roll itself up inside rage and reach its tipping point. Like the kids who stared at the naive curling of my face opposing their declaration that I lived in the projects, I think Keonna felt sorry for me. Except she also cared for me and held empathy for the slow burn scorching a bit more of my dignity each day. She understood it wasn't me who punched her, but the shame.

Fortunate or foolish, ignorance of my family's financial situation was the result of a carefully cultivated, insulated upbringing. I lived in a bubble. When not at home, my days consisted of school, church, and Grandma's house. She lived in a neighborhood called Tarrytown. It was closer to Locke, somewhat nicer and safer. I was in school with kids who lived in her district, just across the border of maximum scarcity. This was one variable in an equation explaining why I was poorer than them.

Sure, I got free lunch at school. Didn't everyone? I saw far more kids hand the lunch lady a punchcard than cash in exchange for their tray of pizza, green beans, applesauce, and chocolate milk. I also made every field trip. No one forbade me from participating in extracurricular activities because of cost. I knew we had less than some. But we had more than others.

I don't ever remember my mother telling me we didn't have money for something. Danny and I didn't receive everything we asked for, and went without amenities like cable television, but if a reason was given, it wasn't insufficient funds.

Our mother made sure we got what we wanted on special occasions like birthdays, and bought us new outfits at the start of each school year. Incredible maneuvering, I'm sure, was required to manifest these small miracles and shield us from the reality that we were members of the have-nots. She also had the support of her village. Her parents, gap-fillers like Grandmama, and my wealthy Chicago aunt who bought me fancy dresses helped further camouflage our economic status.

I knew the absence of a second parent contributed to the poverty of which I had become suddenly conscious. I mean, the couple of times Champ was around, I got sneakers from Foot Locker. When he wasn't, I got the ones from Payless and K-Mart. The ones that served as bullseyes on my feet. The ones kids made fun of. Though until the mocking, I cared little for the difference. I didn't love my old pink sneakers because they were Reeboks, but because of who gave them to me and what I convinced myself the giving represented.

Drugs and drug dealing were on a steady incline, another variable. This was how some of my poverty-adjacent classmates afforded their luxuries. Many of their parents and family members, who didn't work in the steel mills, sold drugs or reaped benefits from those who did. Many single mothers had a boyfriend, a brother, a nephew, a *someone* resigned to getting money by any means necessary. Mine didn't. My mother's boyfriend, Terry, was as straight an arrow as they came.

Terry was another gap-filler, however. Someone who made us forget how much we lacked by making lack less obvious. He and my mother worked in tandem sometimes.

In the same chair where I'd waited for Champ to arrive, I sat unwrapping gifts one Christmas morning. We had a tiny Charlie Brown-like tree, but my mother would gift wrap a huge box and place the decorated tree on top so it seemed taller.

When Danny and I went to sleep the night before, there was nothing under the tree. That's what our mother did, we'd learn. She waited until we were in bed on Christmas Eve to bring out the presents she'd hidden in her closet and at other people's houses over the preceding weeks. She wanted everything to be a surprise. She wanted our sheepish eyes to enlarge when we stumbled into the living room the next morning and saw just how many presents were waiting to be unwrapped. It worked too. There were always more than either of us anticipated.

I sat, curled up in the chair. As I tore into one gift, my mom or Terry handed me another until I was done, and disappointed. Taught to be grateful, I tried to hide it, but a knot went rushing up my windpipe.

There was one thing I wanted more than anything else. A karaoke microphone was all I'd talked about for the past few months. I expected it to be there because my mother always, somehow, someway ensured our wish list materialized on Christmas. We experienced many let downs but never on this day.

Miracles.

I sat surrounded by tattered wrapping paper, watching my apple-head brother have the morning of his life unboxing new remote-controlled cars and action figures. I treasured everything I'd gotten. The dolls, the Teddy Ruxpin, the coloring books were all coveted items. It was just this one thing. This one small thing.

My mother observed my face trying its best to look happy but failing, and asked what was wrong. I pointed my eyes off into the distance. I couldn't say it. Couldn't be a brat.

"Oh, wait," she said. "Something's missing." She rotated her head around the room with exaggerated bewilderment as though she were genuinely puzzled and curious about where the missing item might be.

Terry went into my mother's room. He returned carrying a small, gift-wrapped box and gave it to my mother, who handed it to me.

I knew it! I knew it! The words echoed through my mind as I ripped into my final present. I pulled out the microphone, cheesed and held it high in the air for everyone to see, like a trophy. My mother tilted her head and smiled at the carpet.

I knew it. I knew she'd come through. Her Christmas Day winning streak continued.

I wonder if fathers consider who might assume their abandoned posts. Could be an uncle, a boyfriend, the drug dealer next door, or the predatory old man down the street. I got lucky this time in getting Terry. Who stepped in as needed, even on his own.

The car that pulled into our driveway the day I sat wishing it might belong to my father, belonged to him. As soon as the popup headlights came into clear view, I knew it was his little red sports car. He hopped out and walked into the house while I held my position, motionless.

Terry paused at the entryway and asked why I was sitting in front of the window, alone in our dimly lit living room. I couldn't turn to acknowledge his presence. Yet another person would know I was waiting for someone who had made it clear—if not in the first hour, absolutely by the third hour and unequivocally by this hour—that he did not want me.

I continued pretending something in the street commanded my attention as Terry paused for a reply. A few silent seconds passed before he walked away. I heard him go into my mother's bedroom and ask the same question. "Why is she sitting in front of the window?" They closed the door and whispered.

Terry marched out of the room, over to me, and said, "Let's go." The command was firm. He'd never told me what to do before. Ever the diplomat, he made suggestions and requests, but did not give orders. I stayed quiet but climbed down from the chair and followed him out to his car. He held the passenger side door open as I slid into a gray leather bucket seat.

Terry settled in behind the wheel and started the engine. "Where we going?" I finally gathered enough fresh air to speak. "To get you a bookbag," he answered. I shivered.

Terry looks and laughs like a tall Eddie Murphy. He's well over six feet but boasts the same smile, same voice, same look as the comedy legend. Danny and I lived to do something he found funny to also witness the audible resemblance.

He's not flashy, though. It seemed Terry owned only one pair of jeans, or multiple identical pairs all worn in the knees. He sported the jeans whenever we saw him, with the same pair of plain black sneakers and a fitted, solid-colored t-shirt.

The man was like Grandaddy down to the basic daily uniform. It must've played a role in my mother choosing him. We were all flabbergasted when he drove up one day in the little red sports car with popup headlights. It contradicted his style. Until then he had a gray compact sedan, something practical, like a Toyota Corolla maybe, which matched the frugal driver with simple taste in fashion who stepped out of it.

Terry turned into a Walgreens parking lot. It was one of the few stores still open on a Sunday evening. I skipped through the sliding doors and followed him to the school supply aisle. Notebooks and reams of paper were rifled through and flung about, leaving slim pickings for most last-minute items. But for backpacks, there remained a few options.

Wow, I get to choose! I realized. It was like someone had handed me a golden ticket.

I weighed the pros and cons of each. *This one will get dirty way too easy. That one looks too small for all my books. The black one has a skull on it; Grandma won't like that.* I contemplated which choices other kids might find cool and compared those against backpacks I'd had in years prior.

A bright red-and-blue tote bag with thick, round handles caught my eye. Every backpack I'd ever had went on your back. The novelty of this one felt special.

"Sure that's the one you want?" Terry asked as I handed him the bag. "Yes!" I verified while we walked to the register. My first smile emerged since waking with the belief it would be father-daughter day. Terry responded to it with THE laugh and said, "Okay."

The laugh made me laugh.

We stopped at Dairy Queen on the way home and Terry got me my favorite, a vanilla ice cream cone dipped in cherry. All was right with the world. Well, better, anyway. I didn't have my father, but I'd gotten my bookbag. I didn't start school the next morning carrying the one from a year prior as a reminder of my grief.

Decades would pass before anyone in my household spoke of Champ again. It was as if he had never existed. Adults didn't talk to me about serious things. And aside from Grandma using the words "nervous breakdown" once, no one even discussed San Diego. Maybe they were all protecting my childish fragility and didn't want me to think of things that might make me sad. Maybe my mother couldn't discuss things that made her sad.

I promised myself I wouldn't ask anymore. I'd play along and tuck memories of my father away where they couldn't bother anyone. I'd move on. If someone could please, just tell me what to do when it hurts.

5
In Whispers

I understood early why men were drawn to my mother. Why potential suitors came to her with ease and why, when one person left, it wasn't long before she replaced him with another. After Champ, she married my brother's father so early in my life that I knew him as Daddy. After Daddy came Terry, after Terry came a boyfriend who blurred my lines between man and monster, and after the monster it didn't matter who came. I was done with whomever it was before meeting them.

My mother is an attractive, stylish woman who in her day rocked blown out hair with curled ends that bounced on her shoulders. Sometimes she'd wrap a chic headband around the crown like Farrah Fawcett. She wore all the 80s fashion trends: crop-tops, pedal pushers, and high-waisted, stonewashed jeans. Almost eclipsed by it all, at last you'd notice the application of her signature dark purple lipstick, a flawless outline around her mouth.

Some nights my mother put on her favorite record, "The Lady in Red" by Chris De Burgh, and cranked the volume up.

Her singing voice rivaled professional standards. Danny and I would slow dance with each other's shadows in the living room while marveling at the grace of our mother floating in sync with each instrument and belting out every note. Never had the lyrics of a song seemed such a perfect fit for a person.

While waiting for my mother to pick me up from school, the fathers of other kids would ask about her. I'd stand on the sidewalk gripping my backpack straps, focused on approaching vehicles, before interrupted by the booming bass of a male voice.

"I know whose daughter you are. Went to school witcha momma. You look just like her!"

Danny always stood next to me and sneaked a glimpse in my direction when these monologues ensued. From the corner of my eye I would see his raised eyebrows and the teeth his mouth hadn't yet grown into. Everything was funny to him.

"So, how ya momma doing?" some of the men would continue.

"Had a li'l crush on her back in the day. If she gave me a chance, I'd take care of all y'all. She wouldn't have to worry bout nothin!"

I learned that many men view themselves as the solution to women's problems. I'd avoid eye contact as they talked, deliberating what I was to do with this information. They often ended by instructing me to pass along a greeting. I said I would. Sometimes I did.

When I told my mother, "So and so's father said hi," she just smiled.

"Tell him I said hello."

Despite a hefty selection of men to choose from, casual dating wasn't my mother's thing. She wanted to remarry and gravitated toward long-term courtship. This is why she moved on from Terry a couple years after he salvaged my day spent in front of the window. She left him despite what seemed to me his absolute perfection.

Terry was mild-mannered and methodical. He spoke slowly, like he was choosing each word as he went along, and always moved at the same careful pace. A master at *dad mode*, you wouldn't know he had no children of his own. He also didn't have his own father. How did he learn to excel at the role?

I think Terry emulated the wholesome dads he admired in the family sitcoms we sat on the sofa and watched together. Carl Winslow from *Family Matters*, Uncle Phil from *The Fresh Prince of Bel-Air*. Dr. Huxtable. We felt like those families when Terry was around. Like we were in a show where parents and children spent quality hours together and no transgression was left unlectured. If we watched a movie, he'd have discussion questions ready after. When we played Monopoly, he'd explain our bad financial decisions and how we could've better strategized.

It wasn't all talking and TV watching. When we moved to Concord Village and our home was burglarized every couple of months, Terry protected us. One of those times, burglars broke the deadbolt on our door and damaged the hinges to the point where it couldn't be secured. It was late. With no stores open or repairmen to be found, Terry came over. He asked for a pillow and blanket and slept on the floor in front of the busted door all night. He could've just as well slept on the nearby couch but instead chose a position that made it difficult for anyone to get past him, to make us feel safe. It worked.

The next morning, he went home to get his tool bag and then to the hardware store. Terry returned with a new lock, door hinges, a slab of wood, and metal brackets. After fixing the door, he installed a removable wooden bar we slid in front of it at night to prevent anyone from kicking it open while we were inside.

We'd come home from our daily routines to see he'd cut the grass, sometimes catching him in the act. On trash day, we'd wake to discover Terry had stopped by and wheeled our big green garbage bin to the curb. Terry ate the milk and cookies we left for Santa. We knew it was him. It was always him.

Could life be this way? Could I talk and have someone listen? Could someone handle me with care, keep me safe, and hold me in high regard unattached to anything I'd done to earn it? With Terry, the answer was yes. I didn't know if it was him I loved or the environment, the calming stability he brought to the chaos inside me.

I hoped he'd stick around and asked, "How come you don't want to get married?" He didn't snap or tell me to stay out of grown folk's business.

"I want to get married someday, just not right now," Terry said.

His explanation was logical. Working in the maintenance department at a local elementary school, he wanted to get a better job to support the family he'd inherit. He wanted time to become the man who could meet the standards of husband and stepfather he would set for himself.

A year or two into Terry's relationship with our mother, Danny and I started orchestrating mock wedding ceremonies because we knew what she wanted. We wanted it too. Organizing these trial runs was our way of trying to get Terry on board.

A ring from our mother's jewelry box served as her wedding band. After we had the two of them repeat random vows, my brother or I would hand the ring to Terry. He pretended to tremble with nerves while our mother stretched forth her hand. He exaggerated the trembling and fumbling as he reached the ring toward her. Every time. Every. Single. Time. Just as the faux symbol of commitment touched the tip of his bride's finger, Terry dropped it to the floor. One of us kids would retrieve the ring from the carpet and give it back to Terry. We'd each grab one side of his arm, trying to hold it steady as he made another attempt. To the floor the ring went once more, right when we thought it might reach its destination.

We found the display hilarious. We'd roll on the floor with laughter and try again and again until our mother got tired of the role play. She didn't see any humor in Terry's continued refusal to at least pretend to marry her. The only reason she played along at all, I think, was in hopes that one of those times he'd actually slide the ring down her finger. The action would signal he was warming up to the real thing.

After what she deemed too long, however, my mother was fed up with his procrastination. She was done waiting. Done pressuring. Done with fake, playful ceremonies. She ended their relationship and dove back into the dating pool. The sharks circled.

I understood too that maybe marriage doesn't need to be the goal. That how you're treated matters more than who's willing to walk down the aisle. I'll take actual devotion over a legal document that declares it—but I know my mother desired both.

Dang, no more Terry. It was a sad day when she broke the news. A day sadder, in retrospect, after we met his replacement.

Like everyone, my mother wanted love. But only partners who demonstrated staying power earned the privilege of meeting her children. Earning it, however, does not mean they deserved it.

Kareem said and did all the right things to gain access across that threshold, despite his personality contrasting Terry's at every turn. He was stone-faced and quiet. Not the kind of quiet that appeared meek. The kind that sat seething beneath a clenched jaw waiting to unleash poorly suppressed fury.

Anger gurgled from Kareem's throat when he barked out commands. It made his already raspy voice sound like it was underwater.

"Shut-up!"

"Turn the TV down!"

"Go to bed!"

He said little to me or my brother unless irritated by reminders of our existence.

My mother certainly has a type, because physically, Kareem did resemble Terry. Not as handsome, but he was tall like him. Milk chocolate skinned like him. Had a thick mustache and shag haircut like him. A demented Eddie Murphy doppelganger with a permanent scowl, face rough with straw-like stubble, and lips darkened a deep purple by cigarettes. I don't know if Kareem also shared the laugh because I never heard it.

Danny did the best impressions of people. He did an impeccable rendition of Terry's laugh. He did Grandma's angry face— her lips poked out, her furious stomping around the house—with supreme precision. He might've made jokes and imitated the curmudgeon serving as our mother's new boyfriend. We might have laughed at his frivolous misery had it not filled us with terror.

Instead, we behaved as instructed. We tried to stay small and off Kareem's radar. Especially once we discovered what would happen if we didn't.

It seemed craving a woman can make a man tolerate children he does not want. There were no fun family activities with this boyfriend. No game nights or drive-in movies. Every rare outing turned tragic, like when the four of us came back from Dairy Queen one sticky summer day mere weeks into meeting Kareem.

He did things like this. I don't think he cared much what Danny or I thought of him, but he wanted to impress our mother. He wanted to remain on her good side. So, every now and then Kareem would try to paint himself in a more favorable light. He'd do something that seemed kind on the surface, like taking us to get ice cream. Smashed between days and days of tense interactions, his gestures seemed out of place. And he could never play the *nice guy* part for long.

My mother and brother preferred the Dairy Queen Blizzard,

a thick shake that came in a cup with a lid. I got the soft-serve vanilla ice cream cone dipped in cherry, like always. I don't hold many joyful childhood memories, but my love affair with this specific treat is one of the few. It's how Grandaddy paid me after a day of feeding chickens on his farm. It's what I requested if rewarded for making the honor roll at school or nailing a long speech at church. This is why Terry got it for me after we left Walgreens with my new bookbag. Everyone knew it as my chosen childhood comfort food, my fastest road to happy.

Racing against my ice cream's rapid melting, I exited the backseat of Kareem's powder blue Honda. Licking and slurping and biting into the crunchy red coating garnered my full attention. Lost in the thrill of it all, I didn't look up to remember bees had made a home above the entrance to ours. Focused on the task at hand, I made my way up the driveway. The bees reminded me of their presence by swarming my sweet treat.

I stopped walking about six feet from shelter and looked up at the hive. All its occupants appeared to be making a beeline for me. I let out a scream while everyone passed me by and waited at the door. They were coaxing and coaching me the way you do babies wobbling on their feet, contemplating whether to push one forward.

Squeezing his sweating Blizzard cup, Danny swung his head around and removed the plastic red DQ spoon from his mouth. "It's okay," he said. "Look, they didn't sting me!"

My mother encouraged me with a gentle, "Come on, you can do it. Just run really fast!"

Her new boyfriend was less patient.

"Get in the house!" Kareem snarled.

I heard him but the bees bumbling my way continued commanding my attention. I still couldn't move. Could barely tell I had legs. I didn't know what else to do but cry.

My tears set Kareem all the way off. He could've picked me

up and carried me inside. He could've stood between me and the bees, acting as a shield. He could've offered to hold my ice cream so the bees would divert their attention his way. Terry would've done one of those things. Instead, this strange man rushed over to me, grabbed my free hand, and jerked my arm into the air. WHAM! He slapped me on the butt. Then he slapped again, and again, and again. And again. Every blow pushed me closer to the door.

The first hit took me by surprise. I jumped. The fist clutching my ice cream cone threw it into the air.

My mother yelled, "Kareem! She's scared!" But her rationale was no match for his rage.

The spanking worked. It knocked me out of my trepidation-laced trance and back into the moment. Watching my ice cream cone tumble down and splatter onto the concrete compounded my fear and my shock and the pain radiating from my bottom. I ran wailing inside the house, up the stairs, and into my room where I shut the door and folded into bed.

It was dark outside when a knock at my bedroom woke me.

"Come in," I murmured.

My mother's boyfriend flicked the light on. He was holding another vanilla ice cream cone dipped in cherry. Kareem did this too, sometimes, returned to slap a band-aid over the sight of his destruction—often at the behest of my mother.

I sat up in bed and accepted the replacement treat as expected. He didn't apologize or dare promise change. The trade was made in silence, a second ice cream cone for overlooking what had happened to the first.

At a young age, I also learned about manipulation. That there are men who believe a momentary peace offering should suffice to absolve them of infinite infractions. Kareem and I both knew he'd strike again. The only unknown was who would be the target. Would it be my mother? Whom Kareem forbade from going out with her friends or anyone who wasn't him? He ripped phones from walls when she threatened to call my uncles over to remove him from our home. He tied her hands and feet with the phone's cord so she couldn't leave. Much went on behind the closed door of her bedroom or when Danny and I stayed the night at Grandma's. We never saw any of it, though Kareem would show up with roses or chocolates after each incident. Once, he brought over a life-sized white teddy bear squeezing a plush red heart between its paws and planted it in the corner of my mother's room. Each gift was an attempt at making amends for some horrible thing he'd done—before the next horrible thing he'd do.

At this most unfortunate time, Danny grew afraid to sleep alone in his room. Still living in the projects, in this neighborhood filled with the city's poorest people, residents were regularly beat down in backyards. Sometimes killed. The gunshots, moaning, and police sirens ensured we had no silent nights.

If the outside sounds didn't shake you, the constant break-ins would. Just as we got electronics or other coveted items, each was gone, be it the blue BMX bicycle my brother got for his birthday, our living room TV, or the Nintendo we were gifted one Christmas, we knew the clock was ticking on how long we could enjoy having it in our possession. Hell, a few weeks after Danny's birthday, someone came in and rolled his bike away while he stood in the kitchen washing dishes. It was springtime, when we often left the inside door open to allow a nice breeze to flow through the screen door. I guess we'd forgotten to lock it on this day. Looking into our townhouse from the screen door, you could see the living room, up the stairs, and into the hallway leading to a downstairs bathroom. Danny kept his bike leaning against the wall in this hallway. After finishing the dishes, he rounded the corner out of the kitchen and paused.

"Where's my bike?" he asked himself and anyone who might be listening. "Camey, did you take my bike outside?" He shouted up the stairs, "Mommy! My bike is gone!"

We ran down and over to eyeball the space where his BMX normally sat. The audacity. Whomever it was had come in and rolled it right out of the door, undetected.

Once, we came home to an in-progress evening heist. It was morning when we left, so my mom found it odd that lights were on inside our townhouse. She pulled just over the curb of the driveway, stopped, then turned off the car's engine and headlights. "Shhhh." She placed a finger over her mouth. Minutes later, two guys darted out. One of them was carrying our tiny 20-inch television. They ran into the unit directly behind ours without even glancing our way.

Living in Concord I learned not to carry electronics into the house or emptied boxes to the trash in daylight. The streets were watching. They never missed a signal that we had something worth taking.

My mother had no issue with her eight-year-old son dragging his blue *Transformers* blanket into my room and sleeping on the floor at night. He was witnessing things menacing enough to make grown men cower. It was her new romantic partner who saw the practice unfold and didn't approve.

"Get up!"

Just as he'd snuggled into his space, Danny popped back up.

"Go get in your bed and stop being a sissy!"

Kareem curled his lip, looking down at Danny in disgust. "Running to your sister's room like a little girl."

He watched as my brother lowered his head, clutched the corner of his blanket, and staggered next door. Only once Danny was in his room did Kareem walk away, grumbling.

"Better not happen again . . ."

But we were clever, or so we thought. We hatched a plan

to evade Kareem's wrath. Danny got into his bed at night and would lay awake until prolonged quiet told him our mother and her beau were asleep. He'd tiptoe down to my room in the stillness and take his spot on the cold tile. With the sun, he'd rise and tiptoe back.

One night, Kareem got up to use the restroom positioned on the other side of our bedrooms. My door was closed. If we'd been smarter, Danny would've closed his too. We would've made his defiance more difficult to discover.

My brother being snatched from the floor jolted me awake. I squinted my eyes and peered out into the bright hallway. He was wiggling around in his underwear, trying to dodge the slaps of a belt, yelping with each unsuccessful attempt.

Kareem was holding him with one hand by the wrists he'd smashed together and pinned over Danny's head. His grip was firm; only the lower half of my brother's body swung in whichever direction his legs hopped. He was running in place, skinny lower limbs trying to take off in a sprint.

"Stop!" my mother shouted, rushing past my door. "Leave him alone!" She grabbed Kareem's arm, who finally obliged and flung Danny into his bedroom.

I hoped when Danny's sniffles ceased it meant he'd fallen asleep. Whether or not that were true, he stayed in his room alone the rest of the night. In a large corner space where gunshots echoed louder in his ears than anyone else's.

I understood early the importance of believing people the first time they show you who they are. Don't wait for them to show you again. Because they will.

The next night, Kareem's absence allowed for safe passage to my bedroom floor. We didn't ask where he was, simply grateful he wasn't there. No premeditated scheme was needed.

Danny wrapped himself inside his blanket and sprawled across the tile. I thumbed through my stacked milk crates filled with books and chose one, as I did every night. Reading had become my escape. I'd curl up in the corner of my bed closest to my nightlight and vanish into a Judy Blume story or *The Baby-Sitters Club* adventures. I imagined a life better than this one and sometimes read to my baby brother in whispers until his eyes closed, so that he might dream too.

I suppose this was one of those nights. When Danny rested on the floor next to my bed and stared at the ceiling. And I didn't keep the fantasies that rescued me from reality to myself.

A few days passed. Kareem didn't return to our house with an *I'm sorry* gift for Danny. We gawked out at the driveway from an upstairs window. First observing, then giggling at the now ex-boyfriend. He was sitting on the hood of his car with his head down and one foot resting on the front bumper. R&B love songs blared from the radio in a demonstration of desperate longing. We left the window for a while and came back. He was still there. Luther Vandross, Lionel Richie, and Barry White could still be heard singing their hearts out through the car's rolled-down windows.

We frolicked about the house with a freedom not felt in months that had seemed like years. We played and laughed and watched movies in the living room unconcerned we might make an unknown wrong move and suffer the consequence. We turned on the stereo and danced our silly little kid dances, bopping around on our toes and thrusting our hips. We deemed our shenanigans a *Kareem is gone* party. The end of an era entailing countless beatings and beratings for the offense of being children.

Our mother came down to join the celebration. "Mommy!" Danny shrieked and ran over to the stereo. We put her favorite record on and twirled the night away.

"I did it for you," she tells me when I am much older. "I broke up with Kareem because of how he was treating you and Danny. I didn't care so much about what he did to me."

She'd wilted under the weight of desire, and I worried, *is this what awaits me? Looking just like my momma?* I worried that love was merciless, filled with husbands who destroy, fathers who leave—and that wanting to be wanted invites cruelty. Terry was an aberration, the way he admired my mother. I worried because I understood. Some men pick flowers just to pluck the petals.

6

All Legs

Grandma cheered as she came running from the kitchen into the living room. "GO GO GO!" Wet dough still caked between her fingers. She'd paused in making her community-famous homemade yeast rolls to marvel at Michael Jordan and the Chicago Bulls.

Grandma loved her some MJ. Scottie Pippen too. What an amazing era to be a Bulls fan, especially living in the Chicago area. We witnessed two three-peats and claimed the best player in the NBA as our own.

Whenever games were on, Danny, Grandma, possibly an uncle, maybe a cousin, and I gathered around the big floor-model television. I stretched out across the carpet, belly side down with my elbows bent and chin resting inside cupped hands, glaring at the TV in absolute awe.

The way MJ was the hardest working player on the floor, but still somehow glided across it and through the air with such elegance, was quite a sight. The way his tongue hung out when he was about to do something exciting like dunk on his opponent was hypnotic. Then, the style with which he did it all—the gold chain, the gum chewing, the socks, the shoes. No other player was as cool on the court while also as lethal.

Jordan didn't ugly sweat or look out of sorts. He killed opponents softly, casually, made it look easy. There were jumpers in the face of whomever attempted to guard him, or over multiple outstretched hands. Just when defenders thought they had him trapped, Jordan would slither through and suddenly be at the rim. Everyone in the house yelled and screamed and jumped around, astonished. Sometimes I dreamed that he was me.

Those nights spent watching Bulls vs. Pacers, or Pistons, or Knicks, (or anyone, but especially those teams), turned me into a basketball fan. I have a home video my uncle filmed of me dribbling a soccer ball outside his house. I was all legs. Still am. But eighty pounds and all legs looks a bit different than I do now.

Partially covered in flower-printed spandex shorts, my scrawny legs swiveled into and away from my body as I bounced the ball back and forth, side to side. Bony knees protruding in various directions, I performed my greatest trick for the camera, bending one leg forward and extending the other behind me, then bouncing the ball through the space between.

"See, I'm Michael Jordan's long-lost cousin!" I said to the camera and my uncle. "He's your favorite too, huh?" He chirped back as I continued darting around the driveway, slapping a soccer ball against the concrete, looking much smoother in my head, I'm sure, than in reality.

My elementary school posted information about a girl's summer basketball league. I took it home to my mother and begged her to let me play. We went down to the YWCA and signed me up with a team of fellow soon-to-be sixth graders.

Coach Fisher was a gray-haired man with glasses who wore khakis and a polo shirt every day he was with the team. He wasn't mean but rarely smiled. Coach put us through all kinds of skill development training, like layup lines, shooting exercises, and passing drills. For passing drills, we'd line up along each sideline, facing the person across from us. When Coach blew his whistle, we bent our knees and broke out in a lateral run to each end of the court, throwing chest or bounce passes to the person across from us the entire way. All the while, coach stood watching with his arms folded, studying but offering no feedback.

It may have been the first time I dribbled an actual basketball. It was much easier to grip than a soccer ball or those smooth, colorful, rubber bouncy balls stores would dump into a wire-framed cage and sell for a few bucks. The little bumps, the texture on the basketball, made it easier to control. It felt good brushing against my fingertips when I dribbled or spun the ball around in my hands.

Oh, I was trying all kinds of moves now! I dribbled between my legs, behind my back, and through other people's legs! I was showing OUT. Something about how the ball squeaked against the hardwood, it made me think I was really doing something.

I thought I was pretty good. Again, in my head I was moving across the floor and hanging in the air just as cool as my favorite player. My jump shot looked nice too. I saw myself as one of the stars on the team. Coach agreed and named me to the starting lineup.

After a couple weeks of practice, it was game day. There was no seating at the Y, so spectators watched from a standing-room-only platform lining the four walls above the gym. My mom and a few other family members were there to see me play. "Yeah, Camey!" they shouted as I took the court.

I came out for warm-ups in low-top white Nikes with a neon orange swoosh my mother managed to buy me. I rocked the sneakers everywhere, for everything, with thick socks folded down like MJ. We wore blue T-shirts with *Coach Fisher's Team* printed on the front and our numbers on the back. Black mesh shorts completed the ensemble.

During warm-ups, every shot went through the basket as I navigated the layup line with ease. Like Coach taught me, I tossed the ball right off the square on the backboard. He was right, it's hard to miss when you do it that way. And today I was locked in.

An older girl from my church was on the opposing team. I looked over and waved once I noticed her. She strutted to my side of the court, dribbling a ball with the actual poise I imagined I had. "Ugh," she said. "Your legs are ugly!"

At a loss for words when made fun of, I looked down at my blackhead-covered legs before flashing an awkward smile up at the girl. She laughed and dribbled back to her end of the court. Game time.

Things happen much faster during an actual basketball game than in practice. My blood raced through my body almost as soon as the contest started and things got loud. Everyone was yelling. The cheers of friends and family rained down on us from the platform. Both coaches bellowed instructions. My teammates yelled for the ball or for someone to grab a rebound or to play defense. Orders and voices came from every direction, quicker than I could process. I was dazed trying to keep up. Bug-eyed, I sped up, down, and across the floor waving my arms through the air. When someone passed me the ball, I quickly threw it back to them or to someone else, including players on the other team.

Our rivals were bigger than us and used their size advantage to push us around. We couldn't do anything. Almost all our shots were blocked, and we could only grab a rebound when it fell right into our hands. It was no contest. We were blown out and I didn't score a point or do anything else of record.

My family came down from the platform at the end of the game, smiling. It looked like they wanted to say, "Good job," but I left them with not a single act warranting congratulations. So, they just smiled and patted me on the back. All except Danny. His grin split open. "Why didn't you shoot?" he asked.

My first real game had been a disaster. But I was already looking forward to the next one. We had games every weekend and I was excited to play again, no matter the result or how ridiculous I looked. This is how I knew I loved basketball. It wasn't just a way to emulate MJ anymore. Being on the court, slapping five with my teammates, the *swish* of the ball through the net, it all made me feel something. Plus, I told myself I'd do better next time because I knew what to expect. It would be my redemption game. (It wasn't.)

A few days later I had Grandma take me to a doctor to see if anything could be done about the blackheads on my legs. "Nope," he said, apparently annoyed with us for coming in about such a thing. "They'll probably go away as you get older." He pacified me by prescribing a cream he admitted would likely do nothing. I'd just have to outgrow the harmless skin condition.

The doc was right. But until then I took my ugly, scrawny legs to play in the YWCA league the rest of the season and for one additional summer. My teams never made the playoffs, so our seasons ended early.

I visited my Aunt Niecy in Memphis, Tennessee during the few remaining weeks of summer breaks. My mother either drove us or put me and Danny on a Greyhound bus for the eleven-hour ride. I enjoyed the bus trips, watching interesting strangers, listening to my Walkman, and stopping at random restaurants for food.

Aunt Niecy settled in Memphis after graduating college and marrying Uncle Vincent, who was a native of the city. Things were different in her house than mine. Unlike anything I'd experienced.

She had three children occupying the bedrooms, two girls and a boy all at least five years younger than me. I often slept on the couch. One night, I curled up under the blanket and sheet my aunt spread out for me and watched TV. She came into the living room a half hour or so later. "Time to go to sleep," she said and turned off the television. "We have to get up early."

I went to work with Aunt Niecy at a daycare in the mornings. We had to be there at 6 a.m., the earliest parents were allowed to drop off their kids. Helping with the kiddos was my summer job. I made sandwiches for lunch, took them outside to play, and rocked babies to sleep.

After she turned the television off, Aunt Niecy walked over to me and did something no one had ever done before. She pulled the blanket down from my face and kissed me on the forehead.

"Goodnight."

I melted. And was glad the light from the TV had gone away so she couldn't see.

"Goodnight."

I counted the hours until bedtime every evening, and the days till summer vacation in Memphis every season.

Two years was too long. We had reached the limit of our ability to endure public housing. It was too much for a single mother. Grandma, Grandaddy, everyone was worried about us living amid constant violence and illegal activity. After we came home to the in-progress heist, their concern for our welfare swelled.

When I visited Aunt Niecy the summer before seventh grade, I stayed in Memphis, because we didn't just move to another house; my mother relocated us to the city. We shared a three-bedroom apartment with my Aunt Mona and her two younger boys. Danny slept in a room with them, my mother and I shared one, and Aunt Mona had her own room. A cosmetologist, she was the breadwinner of the household and would come home with knots of cash every day.

I was thrilled to be permanently closer to Aunt Niecy. We started going to her church and everyone was warm and affectionate like her. All the women wrapped their arms around me and loved on me. I thought I might burst from the affection.

Memphis was a different world. The part of town we lived in was clean and quiet. No gunshots or scary men hanging on the corners while I waited for the school bus in the mornings or walked back to our apartment in the afternoons.

Raleigh-Egypt Middle School resembled those I'd seen in movies. There were outdoor corridors and lockers, and a courtyard where we ate lunch. Kids were kids but mostly shuffled to class without incident.

I made a friend right away. Kayla had also just moved to the city and didn't know anyone. She had a twin brother who looked like her with shorter hair.

A guy named Tai liked me. He wore dashikis and wooden jewelry to school and sometimes brought a necklace or bracelet for me. I stopped accepting the gifts because the first time I did, he asked for my phone number, and I wasn't interested in giving it to him. But he kept trying. Kept bringing little trinkets, candy on Valentine's Day and keepsakes for Christmas. Each time I refused a gift I could see him growing more frustrated. Until one day he got fed up and called me a bitch.

"Call me a bitch again," I said. Where I'm from those were fighting words.

"Bitch."

I stood up. Tai was sitting at the desk right next to mine, as always. He stood up. I stepped across the aisle and punched him in his right jaw. He didn't do anything. I punched him in the left jaw. He just stared at me. I stared at him, then looked up to notice the teacher staring at both of us. The entire class had turned their heads and was just looking. No one got up and ran over. No one yelled "Oooooh." The room was dead silent. They were completely unfazed! I felt like I was part of *The Matrix*, like the only person not in on how this world worked.

The bell rang and everyone filed out into the hall. Kayla was waiting for me. "Why did you hit him?" She looked confused. I told her what Tai had called me, and she said, "Oh." Then she laughed. "You reached across and hit him in both jaws! I'm gonna call you Crossfire!"

Then it was over. Tai stopped sitting next to me in class. He didn't speak to me at all or even make eye contact.

I was always the first to arrive back home during the week. My mom and Aunt Mona were working, and the younger kids had to be picked up from school. This gave me about an hour or so in the apartment alone.

One day I came home, dropped my bookbag on the dining room floor and walked into the kitchen. There was an open loaf of bread on the counter. I figured someone must have been rushing and forgot to put it away that morning.

While tying a knot around the bread, I heard the shower running. I picked up the phone and called my mother's job.

"I was just making sure you were at work," I said. "Did Mona go to work today?"

"Yeah, why?"

"Because I think I hear the shower running."

"Get out of there!" my mother ordered. "I'm going to call the police!"

I ran panting from our ground-floor apartment to the other end of the front yard and fixed my eyes on the door to our building. A few minutes later, a police car pulled up, then another, then my mother. She and I stood outside while the police walked through our apartment. They came back and told us it was all clear, but they'd found something.

Our furnace was enclosed in a space right outside the apartment. There was a tiny door inside so we could access it if needed, and one in the hall for maintenance. The lock on the outside door had been broken.

Inside this small space, police found a bag of clothes and some papers.

"This guy just got out of prison," one of the officers said. "He must've been staying in here and going into your apartment when you left for the day."

My mother's mouth dropped. "Well, I'm glad my daughter got out before he saw her."

The officer turned to me. "Did you see anyone come out?"

"No," I said. "Maybe he went out through our patio."

Aunt Mona came home.

"That explains it!" she said. "Food has been disappearing so fast. I'd put leftovers in the refrigerator and the next day the container would be almost empty! I bought a two-liter bottle of Coke, had one cup and then it was gone! I just figured the boys must've been getting hungry in the middle of the night."

Police canvassed the area looking for the guy. Maintenance fixed the lock on the outside door and put one inside, too. I went to school the next day and ran over to give Kayla the rundown. This was more salacious than anything that happened in my old neighborhoods.

Soon though, we were back to our usual community concerns. Moving to Memphis might have been a ploy for my mother to show Terry she was serious about leaving him because a year later, we were back in Gary and they were back together. He helped move us to a house in Tarrytown, right behind Grandma's. A wire fence was all that separated our backyards.

I wanted to stay in Memphis with Aunt Niecy and told my mother as much. When we returned to Gary anyway, I asked her to send me back. She said no. "Summers only." I asked why. She gave no answer I found satisfactory. I went into my room, slammed the door, and cried.

Terry stopped by. After my mother explained to him what had transpired and how I'd been in my room every hour since, I heard a gentle knock on my door.

"Can I come in?"

"Yes."

Terry sat on the edge of my twin bed in the darkness and asked, "How come you don't want to live with your mom anymore?"

"Because she doesn't love me."

"What makes you think that?"

"I don't know." I shrugged, though he couldn't see it. "She just doesn't."

"Your mother loves you a lot," he replied. "That's why she doesn't want you to move. She wants you here with her."

I conceded, and Terry left.

But Aunt Niecy had shown me love and it didn't look like this. I wanted her version all the time. The goodnight kisses and being referred to as "baby" and "sweetie." Being touched, held. She showered it all over me. I'd never felt so spotless.

I let it go. Arguing for the move was pointless. Instead, I laid another brick. My house of resentment was outgrowing me.

7

In The Light

I hope Terry wasn't the only reason my mother moved us back to Gary because their reunion was temporary. He still wasn't ready to marry. He wasn't the kind of guy who would lie, but maybe my mother convinced herself otherwise. Maybe she thought true, tender love and the fear of losing her would push him to act against his logic. If she held this belief, it was unfortunately false. Their romance morphed into a friendship where he came by and mowed the lawn or repaired a hole in the wall from time to time but wasn't with us consistently.

Never mind that though. A college graduate now, my mother could get jobs that paid better than the gas station. I didn't live in the projects anymore and walked into eighth grade with my head held a little higher. The root of my most intense ridicule had been pulled.

What they gone say now? I thought my popular, poverty-adjacent peers might offer me a seat at their table. That after a year they might've forgotten the old me. I could reintroduce myself.

I guess my mother and I both held utopian beliefs about the power of time and distance to transform those around us. Whatever small slice of coolness I once carved out proved unsalvageable. I was only in the cool-kid crowd when we were too young to care about differences. After first or second grade, I was out, and the kids who were still in, remembered. I kept the same two best friends, Candace and Keonna, from fourth grade through middle school. Our short-girl band of misfits stayed together, though I'd have a growth spurt to five foot six and become the tallest member.

Church friends were different. A smaller pool from which to choose meant everyone talked to and hung out with everyone. My mother developed relationships with several church ladies who had children. We all hung out together sometimes. The moms would huddle in the kitchen, have Bible study in the living room, or craft together while us kids goofed around. One set of church friends had a Sega Genesis. We stayed holed up in a room collecting rings as *Sonic the Hedgehog* or launching day-long *Street Fighter* and *Mortal Kombat* tournaments.

These friends belonged to Danny, two brothers. Deon and Dontay looked alike. Most strangers thought they were twins. Each had creamy skin with greenish brown eyes and copper curls atop their heads. They were what we called "pretty boys," too beautiful and seemingly delicate to be lumped in with the rest.

Deon and Dontay's dad had a long Jheri Curl he kept pulled back into in a low ponytail. A police officer, he wore funky, black-rimmed glasses and rode a motorcycle. He asked to pick me and Danny up from Grandma's house one day to take us to Six Flags Great America with his two boys. I thought there was no chance Grandma would approve because he didn't go to church. His wife was someone other members of the congregation admired, however, including Grandma.

Ponytail Dad was quiet, but nice. He bobbed his head to secular music and occasionally quipped something to Deon or Dontay as he drove us almost an hour and a half to Gurnee, Illinois. The songs he played were full of bass that vibrated through the car. It bounced off the seats, the doors, the windows, my body, everywhere. New to my ears, his music sounded good!

Sometimes my mother and aunts gathered their children for a carnival, or a train ride to the Taste of Chicago during summer. But I hadn't been anywhere as elaborate as Six Flags. A theme park, especially one of this magnitude, was something else. *Wow* was all I could think as we pulled into the massive parking lot with its endless rows of cars.

I looked up at roller coasters winding toward the sky. Carts went whirling above, down, and around the track. We could hear screams of crazy people inside the carts from the parking lot.

There were games with huge teddy bears and prizes on display. Rides smaller than the roller coasters were scattered about. Families ate funnel cakes and pizza and cotton candy while mascots danced between them.

Heaven must be like Six Flags, I thought. The ultimate playground, though I'd decided roller coasters were out of the question. Just watching people throw their arms up in the air and plummet from a roller coaster's peak to its valley made me want to vomit. So, nope! Absolutely not. I didn't care what anyone said or how hard they tried to convince me.

I drove bumper cars, got on the carousel and a ride called The Spider with tentacles that lifted you a safe distance into the air while sitting inside an attached car. Once in the air, the tentacles lifted the car up and down as The Spider rotated in a circle, causing the cars to spin. I went into a spaceship that spun much faster than The Spider and made me stick to the wall before its floor dropped from beneath my feet. But when the guys got in line for roller coasters, I waited at the ride's exit.

"What are we getting on next?" I asked Ponytail Dad. He pointed to a modest ride in the area we were walking toward. Great. Something I could enjoy.

Danny, Deon, Dontay, and I horseplayed while waiting in line. We cracked jokes and pushed one another and talked about what we couldn't wait to do next. "Best day ever!" We declared.

The line moved at a slow pace, but finally we'd giggled our way to the front. Pausing at the entry gate, a line of connected red carts with black stripes pulled up. *Wait. This looks like a roller coaster cart.* "This is a roller coaster!" I yelled after figuring it out. Ponytail Dad tricked me. I panicked and backed away, shaking my head. "No, no, no, no. I'm not getting on!"

The guys grabbed my arms as I tried to get away. They pulled me closer. Next thing I knew, I was inside the cart and a lady came to strap me in. She pulled a contraption down over my shoulders and I heard it click into place. There was a small vertical handlebar on each side of the contraption, covering my chest. I squeezed a sweaty palm around each one and closed my eyes.

"Ha! It will be over before you know it," Ponytail Dad said from behind me. Danny chimed in, "You got your eyes closed and the ride hasn't even started yet!" I looked up for a second to see all the dumb boys grinning at me. Deon and Dontay leaned forward to see my face. My sibling, strapped in next to me, turned and gawked. They were enjoying this! Too terrified to snap at them, I closed my eyes again.

Heart racing, on the verge of a breakdown, I tried to go someplace else in my head when I felt the cart jerk into motion. It was moving slowly. All I heard was clink, clink, clink. For a millisecond I peeked from beneath my eyelids. The cart was trucking up a hill to the roller coaster's peak, the way I'd witnessed all day in horror. There was no way I could watch what was about to happen.

The cart stopped. Then it felt like it came loose from the track. Like it was out of control, falling straight down. The force lifted me from my seat and pushed my body forward. *I'm being thrown from the cart!* I was certain. My face was tight, pulled backwards. My stomach, hollow, as though there were no longer a stomach there at all.

Everyone screamed and laughed while my eyelids were squeezed together so tightly it almost hurt. Surely there would've been tears if the wind whipping across my face didn't dry them all away. I could only pray it would be over soon.

We reached the bottom and the track leveled out. I was still inside the cart. What a relief.

"Look, Camey!" Deon shouted. His voice rumbled through the air as though he were yelling into a fan. "This part isn't bad!" Everyone encouraged me to open my eyes. Once able, I did. My trust in them had waned, but they were telling the truth.

The roller coaster was called The Demon. Grandma would've had a fit. It was moving super-fast, though the speed and looping didn't bother me as much as the drop.

The Demon jerked around a corner and into a dark tunnel with low, colorful lights. The voices of all kinds of ghosts and goblins echoed through the space but didn't scare me. It was pretty cool. Just as I settled in and got comfortable, the ride was over. Exactly as Ponytail Dad said it would happen.

We slowed to a stop right back where we started. I hopped out of the cart exuberant and confident. "Man, that wasn't nothing!" I bopped around like the Queen of Six Flags, getting into the faces of Danny and his friends, waving my hand at The Demon in a dismissive notion while proclaiming I could "do that all day."

"Want to get on another one?" Ponytail Dad asked. I shut up. But my accomplished smile remained.

There was school me and church me. With Deon, Dontay, and other sanctified peers, I fit. I was one of them. Back amongst my fellow public schoolers, however, I was the same awkward nerd who barely talked. I did dress a little better, however. I'd get a pair of Nikes for the year. Even an irregular pair of Filas sufficed. They were black suede hi-tops. Gorgeous, despite the Fila symbol being on the inside of one shoe and the outside of the other. I kept my ankles crossed when I could remember. But the sneakers were still Filas, still a popular brand name all the other kids were sporting. The irregularity only slightly diminished my pride in wearing them.

Humble beginnings make you grateful for even modest come ups. I still wasn't on the level of kids who got every style of Jordans released and paired the designer sneakers with matching jerseys or Starter jackets. I felt better though, not standing out for all the wrong reasons. Not having other kids call out the "buddies" on my feet.

Even through her reiterating the unimportance of labels, my mother understood the ramifications of being a child outcast. She empathized when kids jived on me, which is why, when I called her from a payphone at school, upset because the kids were calling me Whoopi Goldberg, she came to get me instead of trivializing the concern.

A couple of weeks earlier, she'd paid to have my hair done. The stylist straightened my long, coiled locks and used a crimping iron to add deep waves. It was beautiful and bouncy. I got so many compliments at school. Wesley Williams, the cute lip-licking boy from my fifth-grade class, kissed me, and I was silly enough to let it go to my head. Of course, I asked to have my hair styled the same way again a couple weeks later when all the crimps had gone flat. I wanted to bask in this new light as long as I could. But paying a stylist again so soon wasn't feasible.

My mother said she could do my hair the same way herself. She tried. She could not. The result was by all accounts an afro with very small crinkles you could see if you got close enough.

I was skeptical heading into school, knowing the style didn't look quite like what prompted all the previous praise. Merciless mocking started with Wesley grimacing at my hair before announcing, "You look like Whoopi Goldberg!" The class exploded in laughter as others confirmed, "She does!" They called me by her name the rest of the morning. Between classes, someone would pass me in the hall, point to my hair and holler "Whoopi!" in my direction.

I bear no resemblance at all to the actress. The dig was specific to my hair and only my hair. Because no middle schooler wants to be told they have the hairstyle of a forty-year-old woman whose character in the movie *Ghost* exudes extravagant fashion faux pas.

I think my mom knew the hair I carried to school was suspect. It wasn't a nice, shapely afro. It was an afro clearly supposed to be something else, flying out to the sides with random curls and mini ruffles. My mother knew she was the reason kids were calling me Whoopi Goldberg. Surely, part of the reason she picked me up from school early, without objection, was to own her part in the catastrophe.

I returned the next day with my regular hair, in my regular place, invisible, how I liked it. Standing out at school was dicey. I decided I'd rather stay in my lane, where I knew what to expect.

We experienced bouts of joy, my mother and me. Interludes between disappointments, like when we danced to "The Lady in Red." Like Christmas. Another came when she took me to my first concert. It was an outdoor music festival featuring several acts, but the only one I remember seeing was TLC. I remember them because I'd never seen anyone like them. The animated bravado, the candor, and the unapologetic nature of their presence captivated every pulse in attendance.

It wasn't just that T-Boz, Left Eye, and Chilli had the audacity to flaunt neon condoms across their exteriors. It wasn't only because they were draped in bold, wildly oversized clothing that hung below their waists and seemed to care nothing about being "ladylike." It was the defiant enthusiasm with which they did so. I was fascinated by the display.

No one would make them be small and quiet. I could just tell. No one would push them into the background.

The trio had something I wouldn't have for a long time. Something I'd never witnessed at age thirteen, certainly not among young women.

Weightlessness.

Their whimsical passion overflowed to invigorate not only me, but a city thirsty for exaltation.

I saw the group perform at Gilroy Stadium. The football field doubled as an event venue initially designed to hold 10,000 people. It was declared done in 1956, though space was cleared for an eight-lane running track and a parking lot, both left unpaved. Plans for additional bleachers, restrooms, and concession stands never made it past the blueprints.

Still, the city's symbol of hope was open for business and hosted everyone who was anyone in the area. There was a local talent competition in 1965, won by hometown kids, The Jackson 5. Even the great Stevie Wonder came through for a performance a few years later.

By 1993, however, the Rust Belt devastation was peaking. Gary's expanding reputation as iniquitous territory ballooned after it was named the U.S. murder capital. We never expected anyone of note to bother with us, though someone bothering with us is often exactly what helps sustain residents of towns like ours. It is carnivals, block parties, and citywide picnics that offer breaks from despair. Music festivals and celebrity appearances lift us up. Because if people who matter know we are here, maybe it means we matter too.

What TLC brought into Gilroy defied the ideas I'd developed about life—that it's hard, dangerous, and everyone is angry. They seemed impossible.

Whatever might be occurring outside the event seemed of little relevance, because inside, there was magic; and we unlucky ones who felt fortunate on this day got to hold it.

Gilroy also hosted a KKK rally in 2001, just as the decaying, still half-done site was set to be condemned. I suppose even a field of dreams can't outgrow its environment. Grandma campaigned for mayors who wouldn't allow such things. Residents protested, wrote letters to city officials. But the best efforts of upstanding citizens could not derail the destructive train rolling through.

The stadium continued to sit in ruin once deemed unsafe and shut down. Overrun by untamed flora and marred by failing infrastructure, it became even less than the underdeveloped version of its vision. Gilroy served as a quintessential reminder of the lesson our community learned early and often—most promises go unfulfilled. But if we can make do with what we have, we may steal moments where it feels like enough. At that festival, we stole one such moment.

Concertgoers breathed carefree air the day TLC demonstrated for us joy as a form of resistance. I walked across the green grass, planted myself atop unforgiving bleachers and bore witness to both the performance and those absorbing its energy. I caught a glimpse of my mother and her sisters daring to be happy. Out loud. They laughed from their bellies and twirled from their souls. They hugged themselves and each other, swaying along to "Baby-Baby-Baby." These astounding women, figures of resilience forsaken by the fathers of their children, got to be soft. They got to be filled with self-assurance by three unabashed female singers. No one spoke of their overdue light bills or neighborhood nightmares.

Local OGs, like my uncle wearing his leather motorcycle vest with no shirt underneath and boot-cut jeans, bobbed their heads to the rhythm of songs belonging to a generation they probably didn't understand. Small children ran around in circles, screaming and giggling with no regard for the racket. Kids remembered they were kids and weary humans laid their burdens down. People got to see how they might look in the light and I thought for a second that maybe dreams do come true because I believe we all saw a waterfall we might wish to chase that night.

Like the stadium holding it, our joy was left unfinished. We would go back to our uninspiring routines and perpetual challenges. But for at least a thirty minutes or so, everything was alright. The old felt young, and the young felt free.

8
Too Late

My mother selected someone fresh from her garden of potential suitors. When she introduced us to her new boyfriend, he seemed fine. Danny and I thought him to be youthful, rather cool. He pulled up in a red box Chevy with speakers in the trunk, just like the hip twenty-somethings in our neighborhood. The new boyfriend stepped out of the car wearing overall shorts with one strap undone and dangling past his waist. He wore his overalls just like us! To top it off he had on thick socks and black hi-top Nikes, the Deion Sanders style. Sneakers didn't get much trendier in the 90s. Aside from Air Jordans, all the kids wanted Deion Sanders or Bo Jackson hi-tops.

Mouths agape and faces scrunched with confused fascination, we said hello as my mother brought him into our home. "Guys, this is Richard." His voice was soft and hoarse, almost like he was laboring to use it, with a hint of southern twang. He pronounced *here* as *her.* Like, "I'm glad I could come over *her* and meet y'all." It was excellent material for Danny's still accurate impressions.

After exchanging basic pleasantries, my brother and I retreated to our bedrooms. A little while later I came out and headed toward the kitchen. The sight I witnessed stopped me before entering. I stood there, unable to look away. My mother was sitting in a chair at the kitchen table. The cool new man was bent toward her with a finger beneath her chin, tilting it up toward him. They were kissing. Kissing for a while. Kissing so long they didn't notice me watching from the hallway. They were kissing when I got there and still kissing when I recoiled back to my room. It was the first time I remember seeing my mother demonstrate affection beyond a quick hug or pat on the back. I supposed she must love him to openly engage in such behavior.

We went to Richard's house sometimes, where he'd put on a movie the four of us would watch together. He and my mom cuddled up on the couch while Danny and I sat cross-legged on the floor. Any time Richard left the room, my brother used it as his opportunity to imitate him.

"Caaame," he'd start in an exaggeratedly strained voice. "Could you pass the remote over *her*?"

"Stop it," our mother would instruct between giggles.

It was all in fun. Richard seemed okay enough. He wasn't Terry but he also wasn't Kareem. His personality fell somewhere in the middle, nice but not very talkative. That he seemed concerned with our well-being, always asking if we wanted anything like blankets, soda, or more popcorn, made the space at least feel safe.

Just a few months later, my mother married Richard in a ceremony without fanfare. They'd both been here before. The focus was on vows, rings, and the intertwining of lives, not the number of witnesses or the extent of elaborate attire. I mean, we were cute. She was still my crafty, fashionable mother after all! But nothing was over the top.

After the service, Danny and I lined up for pictures next to our new stepsisters and stepbrothers, two of each. One girl was fifteen like me, the other was thirteen like my brother, with the boys a few years behind. Despite our closeness in age, we were noticeably different. My stepsisters immediately referred to me as their sister and my brother as their brother. They cared about family. It meant something to them. They wanted to talk and be friends and hang out.

Though my step-siblings grew up in the Gary region, all except one had moved about three hours away to Terre Haute, Indiana with their mother. The other was a decade younger than me and lived nearby with his mom. Distance made developing any type of relationship with the older kids seem senseless. It was enough of a struggle to bond with those living in my household, people I saw every day. I couldn't conceive of it happening with anyone I interacted with infrequently. When they came and stayed with us during summer, Danny hung out with them, but not me.

It was too late for a lot of things, like having another stepfather when I still carried the surname of the last one, and had also attached myself to Terry. Richard called me "daughter," took us on family outings and did no harm. He would've done anything for me if I'd allowed him. If I'd only asked. But I was an attitudinal teenager set in my guarded ways. I didn't want to need anything from him. Ever.

My stepfather tried to make his presence felt, though I resisted making space. I'd come into the house and not speak, zipping straight to my room where I stayed quite literally unless needing to use the bathroom, shower, or eat. He pretended not to care or notice. Or maybe he wasn't pretending. Richard was just that easygoing. He'd continue staring at the TV when I came in, as though unaware I'd entered the room. He made the moments less awkward, less demanding of us both.

Sometimes he'd try to joke and laugh and talk. I'd flat-out ignore the attempt. I was raised to not be disrespectful, but I was every bit of indifferent.

Every fallacy. Every argument he had with my mom. Everything I ever knew Richard did that perhaps he shouldn't have done was used against him in the court of my mind. Loving him or letting him love me wasn't an option. I interacted with him only when unavoidable. We'd go weeks in the same household, exchanging barely a few words.

Still, Richard didn't hold my coldness against me. He kept referring to me as "daughter" and himself as "dad." On the rare occasion I did come to him for something, he sprang into action, no questions asked. "Dad will be thurr. Dad will take care of it." He smiled when the job was done. When the desk was assembled, or the tire was changed, or the heavy item was carried into my bedroom, he radiated with pride. "Thurr you go daughter."

Danny called Richard "Pops." Always the warmer and more inviting child, he embraced having another parental figure dropped into our lives. He embraced having a man around. Love and relationships came easier for him.

My brother entered the house after school and went out of his way to peek around the corner, through the kitchen and into the living room to shout, "What up, Pops!" before heading down to the basement.

We had a basement now. With two incomes, we moved to an even nicer poverty-adjacent neighborhood, initially considered a suburb of Gary. Its residents were more affluent and thus the area was less riddled with crime. Houses were newer and larger. The Glen Park home my mom and Richard bought had four bedrooms, two bathrooms, a basement, and a huge backyard.

Before we moved, my mother was already sending me across town to Lew Wallace, the high school in Glen Park, so I didn't need to transfer. My aunt worked there and was able to get me in despite my not living in the district. She picked me up on her way to the school every morning of freshman year.

Danny wanted to know why I dismissed our stepfather, who was nothing but nice to us. Just as he interrogated me about why I detached from Daddy, who was back in our lives after the Navy stationed him a little over an hour west of Gary in Great Lakes, Illinois a few years before our mother remarried. On weekends Daddy came and stayed in Gary with his mother, Grandma Lilly.

We still didn't know quite what happened in San Diego or why. My brother and I had no understanding of how insufferable a human Daddy had been to our Mommy. If we had known, how could we have gone on loving him? Yet I, gifted at pushing people away, found other reasons to withdraw.

Daddy continued to treat me the same as he did his son. He'd pick us up to stay with him at Grandma Lilly's for the weekend. She'd stop smoking her cigarette and flash gold teeth through a wide smile whenever we came through the door. She, too, treated me as though I were still hers.

Danny and I hung out in a spare room watching movies like *The NeverEnding Story* while Daddy relaxed on the living room couch. Sometimes we'd make popcorn and he'd let us watch his movies, stuff we weren't allowed to see at home, like *Beverly Hills Cop* and *I'm Gonna Git You Sucka*. Visits with Daddy felt like sneaking away with the fun parent. He and Grandma Lilly drank liquor, and we all laughed at things condemnable in my household. He gave me my first sip of beer, which assured I wouldn't want another for a long time.

If Daddy took Danny shopping for school clothes, he took me. We went to the store on his military base where he got discounts. He took us both to see movies and eat at restaurants. He made valiant efforts to revive our daddy-daughter dynamic.

It was me who complicated the interactions. Me, who felt the discomfort of knowing something I could not unknow—I was not his little girl. Not anymore. Not by marriage or otherwise.

I started declining invitations to hang out or go see Grandma Lilly altogether. I'd stay home when he came to get Danny, not stepping outside to even say hi. He didn't stop trying though.

Daddy would ask Danny what was wrong with me. He'd call to talk, and I'd feign busyness. On the rare occasions I couldn't escape a conversation, I'd tell him everything was fine and commit to going with him next time. Next time became the next time. Then the next time. By age fifteen, I had no plans to join him on weekends or holiday excursions ever again.

Everything wasn't fine. But I didn't know exactly what was wrong, so I didn't know how to fix it. Daddy never came into our house, before or after my mother remarried. He pulled into the driveway and honked. I stayed locked inside my bedroom when he arrived. Danny would knock on the door and ask me to come. "Daddy wants to see you," he'd say. Sounding more desperate with each attempt. Once he accepted the ineffectiveness of his efforts, he ran out to the car alone.

When my sweet sibling saw me doing the same thing with our new stepfather, he couldn't understand. He wanted to know why I didn't talk to Richard. Danny never understood. His mind, free from self-preserving walls, couldn't grasp why one would reject another's goodness.

My brother wanted answers, like always. Like always, I had none. I only knew I wanted to be left with my apathy. Left in the solitude thrust upon me because it felt better than hoping the people around me would stay. Or that those who were supposed to love me, someday would. I put my foot in the revolving door of father figures, stopped it from spinning. Whatever part of me once wanted one, didn't anymore.

9

Say Stay

Candace, Keonna, and I broke up. Our *Li'l Bit* clique was hard to keep intact with me not attending West Side, the high school zoned for Tarrytown. It got even more difficult once I moved away. We talked on the phone some, then less and less until we didn't talk at all.

I had to make new friends. The thought terrified me. But the chance to reinvent myself was exciting.

Freshman year I hung out with the one person I knew at Lew Wallace, an upperclassman who went to my church. Kicking it with her showed me I wasn't the only person whose church self was very different from their school self. At school she was even more reserved and afraid to talk to other students than me, far from the authoritative personality I'd come to know. We ate lunch by ourselves, behind the school.

She didn't go to sock hops, basketball games, or any extracurricular events. It was fine at first, but I wanted the true high school experience my sophomore year. New environment, new people, no history of humiliation; I wanted to try and make good on my fresh start.

Gary was full-out Garying by tenth grade. We nicknamed Lew Wallace "El Dubb" or simply "The Dubb". Whether it was better than high schools entrenched deeper in the hood became debatable. Similar violence seeped across assumed lines. Regular fights erupted in the halls like at every other school. Our quarterback was accidentally shot and killed by his best friend. Others were shot and killed on purpose.

Nothing about street life intrigued me. I suppose after being insulated inside church and Grandma's house most of my years, I couldn't normalize it. I wasn't ever attracted to the money flashed by D-Boys or gangsters, and dated regular guys, even a few nerds. Yet my first puppy-love relationship was with a drug dealer named Eric. I didn't know he was a drug dealer though, until he showed up to school in a Cadillac Seville. We called those "shorty boys" because they weren't long like other models.

Can you imagine? A fifteen-year-old with no driver's license and no job rolling in a Caddy? It's quite ridiculous, but was our normal.

Eric wasn't traditionally handsome, but cute in his own way. Better, he was funny, which made him cuter. He was a goofball with a toothy smile who made people laugh.

His mom was a beautician and made sure Eric's hair stayed freshly cornrowed or finger waved. He called me "shawty" and always smelled sooo good. His scent was clean and crisp, like he'd just taken an Irish Spring shower. All these things combined made me like him, a lot.

When we met we were both quiet, quirky kids to whom no one paid much attention. Most days, Eric came into English class and laid his head down on his desk the entire hour. His silliness was reserved for intimate settings, such as when we were split into smaller groups for in-class projects. Here, he shined. I saw him, and he saw me.

We each grinned at the other when one of us spoke. I'd be looking at someone else in the group, discussing the project, and see his teeth out of the corner of my eye. When I turned to face him, he kept cheesing, making no attempt to hide his fondness. When it was Eric's turn to contribute, he opted to crack a joke or read from our textbook in a weird voice and send the group howling. I teased him for it, told him to stop, but it was clear I didn't want him to.

"Lemme get your number, shawty," Eric jogged up behind me and said after class one day. I pulled an ink pen from my backpack and wrote it on his hand.

"Bet. I'ma call you tonight." He tucked the hand into his leather jacket pocket. I walked away and turned to see that he was watching, smiling.

I sat by the cordless phone in my bedroom as soon as I got home from school. Once Eric called, we talked the rest of the night. As conversation wound down, he asked, "Will you be my girlfriend?"

I knew the frivolous nature of boys, how one kissed me when my hair was beautifully crimped in eighth grade but went back to jiving on me when the hairstyle went awry. "I think we should talk on the phone for two weeks, and then ask me again," I answered.

"Okay. I can do that," he said. And he did.

We talked late into the night, every night. Well, we tied the line up, anyway. Some of that time was spent talking, the rest we spent breathing into each other's ears while he played video games, or I did homework.

"You still there, shawty?" Eric asked every now and then. Or, "What are you studying tonight?"

We were better in person, joking and laughing about

random things at school. Eric was different on the phone. When I asked questions, he gave brief responses.

"How was school?"

"It was cool."

"How are you feeling today?"

"I'm straight."

He never went into detail about anything but would listen to me ramble on about my favorite subjects, songs, and movies until I ran out of things to say. This was enough for me. I equated his listening with caring.

"Hold on," we said and sat the phone down when needing to step away. Sometimes I heard him talking to his mom in the background or feeding his dog. We didn't hang up unless we had to—which was often when my mother picked up the phone in her bedroom and interrupted our conversations with, "I need to make a call," or, "Time for bed." I never knew how long she'd been listening before speaking.

"I hate when she does that," I told Eric.

"It's all good, shawty," he said. "I'll call you at the same time tomorrow."

We played the *who's going to hang up first* game for a minute, but it was always me. I had to hang up before my mother jumped on the line again.

At the end of the fourteenth day he reminded me. "It's been two weeks. Well?"

"Okay," I said. "I'll be your girlfriend."

From then on, Eric walked me to classes, carried my books, and bought me candy from the corner store. He brought chocolates and a teddy bear to school on Valentine's Day. On the rare occasions I had to walk home, Eric walked with me even though he lived on the west side of Glen Park, only about a five-minute stroll from school, and I lived on the east side, at least twenty minutes away.

Then my boyfriend showed up in the shorty boy and everything changed. It was clean, a shiny silver with gray leather interior, electric windows and seats. He'd cruise past the school blasting music from the speakers in his trunk and turn every head in the vicinity. He pretended not to notice everyone noticing him with one arm folded, resting outside the window, and the other gripping the steering wheel while his driver's seat was reclined as far back as it could possibly go. He looked straight ahead wearing a baseball cap and dark shades we called Locs, bobbing his head along with Master P or Twista.

The Cadillac was of no interest to me. I rarely got into it, but Eric took me for a few rides, sometimes to get lunch, other times to give me a ride home from school. Each ride was filled with more and more awkward silence. He stopped being funny and appeared angry or anxious all the time.

We were drifting apart and no longer knew how to relate to one another, not even in person. As Eric's money grew, his reputation followed. He started coming to class sporadically. When he did show up, he was the life of the party, talking and joking with everyone, not just me. Girls who'd paid him no attention before started to like him. He liked them back.

Soon, Eric was dating more street-savvy girls who could do things I couldn't and weren't afraid of his lifestyle. They were attracted to his money, the gold chains and diamond earrings he started wearing. My largely good girl, childlike mentality wasn't compatible with this latest, flashy, shorty-boy-driving version of him.

No one called off the relationship. We had an unspoken understanding it was over, and passed each other in the halls like strangers. Sometimes I'd catch Eric standing in a corner with his arm around a girl. Or pulling out a wad of cash, thumbing through a few bills and handing them to her. I'd see him but pretend I didn't. If direct contact was inevitable, he'd scurry past me using one hand to hold up his oversized jeans and offer a greeting. "What up, shawty!"

"What up?" He said it like I was nobody. Like I was some random casual acquaintance. Like we didn't sneak away from school during lunch a few weeks prior and walk to his house, where he laid me across his twin bed and blast-ed 2Pac from a boombox while pushing his way inside me. The experience wasn't memorable for either of us. It was my first time. The pain was intense, like trying to hammer a nail through the eye of a needle. After a few minutes, we gave up. I still thought it meant something though. On our way back to school, Eric walked at least six feet ahead. That should've been the sign he was done with me. Consider-ing how things went after, maybe there was another girl he feared would see us. Or maybe I'm making excuses and he simply was no longer compelled to hide the jerk beneath his charm.

More adept at letting people go with no urge to say stay, I allowed him to disregard me this way. Said nothing. Once I walked through the school's heavy brown doors, he'd al-ready vanished. The vast foyer was completely empty, ex-cept for me, quietly shuffling to my next class and hoping I wouldn't get caught. It's almost what I expected—to again do the thing I did to make people stop loving me.

A noticeable distinction in our new neighborhood was that a lot of kids had fathers in their households. Some still didn't, but all four of my high school best friends lived with both their parents. Three of their fathers were fortunate enough to hold some of the remaining coveted spots in the steel mills. The other worked as a truck driver. All above average incomes.

Luckily, I didn't have to find the new friends I desired because they found me. The first sat behind me in geometry class. Kasey knew people and talked to everyone. One day she started talking to me and we hit it off. She invited me to lunch where I met her two best friends and from then on, we each had three. Senior year I would meet my fourth best friend but until then, this was my circle.

I had not only a friend or two by default, but a group of friends who chose each other. We chose each other every day, for every outing, every secret, every opportunity there was to choose. No one did anything without the others, except when they did things I wasn't allowed to do, like going to house parties, or activities on Sundays while I had to attend church.

I loved Kasey, Iris, and Kim from the time I met them for not making me feel like I had to earn their love. Their friendship and inclusion were given freely. Any fear I held of being discovered undeserving, they put to rest. They kept being there, kept including, kept picking me, and god how it put my abandonment insecurities at ease. How it calmed my anxious efforts to not be a weirdo. I didn't need to do or be anything or dress a certain way for acceptance.

It was my earliest unconditional relationship, my lesson in learning you can have a great love story without romance. My girlfriends were my soulmates. If any one of us got a boyfriend, he would have to fit into our dynamic, not the other way around. None of us ever coupled up with a guy and went missing or became noticeably less available. Our friendship always came first.

It is an extraordinary privilege to have people who won't let you fall or leave you behind. People who save space for you, ensure you aren't treated like an afterthought, and don't merely tolerate but revere your presence. My friends constantly embraced me as-is, and I would never again be who I was before meeting them. Not in the sense of believing I should exist in shadows. We stood out. We dressed alike, talked loud, and laughed louder.

"We used to call y'all the Goof Troop!" A classmate would later reveal. "But not because of you. It was that other one."

We were a troop, was all that mattered to me. We traveled around school in a pack. When the girlfriend of my Cadillac driving ex-boo aggressively questioned me about whether I still talked to him, my friends formed a ring around us. Seeing I was protected, she left me alone.

Hanging with my besties ranked above all things. None of them cared about sports much, let alone played any. So, although Lew Wallace had a girls' basketball team, giving me an opportunity to reclaim what last brought me joy, I didn't think to join. My friends would have cared for me if I wasn't around as much. If I were practicing and playing on weekends instead of at the mall or movies with them, I'd have remained a member of the squad. They would have come to my games and acted a fool in the stands. I just preferred to be where they were, snuggled in my newfound sense of belonging. I traded my sneakers for sanctuary.

My mother was slowly loosening up and allowing me to attend some indoor after-school events, but with one condition: I had to stay with my friends. The four of us wore matching white airbrushed sweatsuits to a boys' basketball game. We only went to the game to be seen. Each of us had the face of our celebrity crush painted on the front of our hoodie. I had Romeo from the group Immature, Iris had Daddy Mac from Kris Kross, Kim had 2Pac, and Kasey had Method Man from the Wu-Tang Clan. On the butt of our sweatpants, we airbrushed "Bow Down" in black cursive letters with a purple border. That Ice Cube song was in heavy rotation and had us feeling tough.

Kim was the feisty one of the crew. At five-foot-two, she was also the shortest. Coincidence? During the game, we happened to sit near a couple of girls who'd been giving her trouble at school. Nasty looks, snickering and pointing when she walked past, stuff like that. It had something to do with Kim dating one of their ex-boyfriends. The four of us agreed we wouldn't say anything unless they said something to Kim first, unless they stepped to her. All was well until we'd walked around showing off our matching sweatsuits enough and decided to leave the game. We made our way down the bleachers when Kim stopped, turned back to the girls, pointed at her butt and said, "Bow down."

"What?" one of them responded. Our eyes widened. This wasn't the plan, Kim! "Bow down. Bow down." She just kept saying it in between hysterical laughter as we dragged her the rest of the way down the bleachers.

When we reached the floor, I looked back up at the girls. They were standing and squinting their eyes at Kim. A few seconds passed before they started making their way down. We kept walking, and Kim sneered at them as we exited the gym.

Outside, we made our way to the car Iris' dad let her drive despite her not having a license. "Kim! Why did you do that?" Kasey and Iris asked. Laughter was all she offered in return before saying something along the lines of, "Because who do they think they are?" She was amused! While we were confused, looking at one another and shaking our heads. But maybe she did it because she knew what I knew, that right or wrong we'd always be there for her. We would not ever leave her to navigate a single struggle alone, even those of her own making. There was comfort in the certainty we wanted her to have. One we all had. Still, we'd often scold her about unnecessarily exercising the privilege.

We all got jobs at McDonald's. Kasey and me first, later Kim and Iris who both had parents who bought them everything they wanted and were totally fine without working. It was about the fellowship for them. I was excited to be able to buy sneakers and FUBU jerseys, and maybe get a car someday.

After handing me two sets of polo shirts and khakis, the manager asked if I could start immediately. She was desperate for help, but I needed to show a legal form of identification before working my first shift. My birth certificate was the only item I possessed from the list. Apparently, the school ID with me sporting a gold Lew Wallace Hornets t-shirt and bleach blonde hair extensions wouldn't suffice.

Procrastinating, I waited until my first scheduled day of work to gather the required credentials. My mother held on to important documents for me. Since she was at work, I went rifling through a filing system of stacked folders and paperwork on the floor next to her bed. She couldn't tell me exactly where the birth certificate was when I called her, only that it was "mixed in there somewhere."

It didn't take long for me to spot the mint green form sandwiched between tax returns and bank statements. I unfolded it. It was my birth certificate, but not the one I was looking for or one I even realized existed.

The last name read *Wilson*. I'd never known it to be mine but knew the name belonged to Champ. The man who'd removed himself from my life almost a decade prior, shortly after entering. I wasn't aware until now there was any record of my once belonging to him. That he came to the hospital to officially claim me and then refused. It had been easier to believe he never committed to being my father than to consider what might've changed his mind.

Seeing *Wilson* on my birth certificate all those years later resurfaced my feeling of being trapped between the worlds of love and obligation, a psychological crawl space I would revisit indefinitely. I slither into it when I'm lost, when I'm angry, when I want to hide. I go to this place where there is room for no one except me.

There was another green half-sheet of paper mixed into the pile of documents. I opened it and saw the last name I recognized. It's the one I share with Danny, the name belonging to *his* father—who I also believed to be mine for a blissful little while.

I remembered how I often forget I'm adopted. This isn't a unique circumstance, I'm aware. Kids are adopted every day and build healthy, loving relationships with their adoptive parents. Perhaps if I viewed my situation this way, and the man who conceived me as merely my birth father, I wouldn't have felt disconnected from the father to whom the baton of responsibility had passed.

Not having gone through a traditional process altered the way I saw things. I wasn't chosen based on my own merit. My adoptive father didn't meet me and say, "She's who I want to be my kid." He fell in love with my mother. He married her. I saw myself as part of the package by default. Now with the package ripped apart, I didn't see myself at all in its pieces.

"You and your brother don't have the same father?" other kids would ask.

"No."

"Oh, so you guys have your mother's last name?"

"No."

"Well, how do you have the same last name?"

"Well, why didn't your mother change it?"

"Well, where is your real father?"

I don't know. I don't know. It's weird. I know. I'm tired. Of these questions.

Even some family members believed I shared a father with Danny. They just assumed. It was mostly outsiders who asked questions. Never my friends though. Such details were irrelevant to them.

Surprises like my Daddy not being mine, like this secret birth certificate, Champ once recognized as my father—it's all made me question what's true. I know nothing and am no one's. Only my friends feel like home. Before them, I'd lost count of how many sleeps it'd been since I'd felt safe.

10
Cool Adjacent

Iris left McDonald's only a few paychecks after starting. Kim was fired. Or she quit. The order and exact framing of events here is unclear, but once you toss frozen hamburger patties to the floor and curse out your manager, the result is the same no matter the initiator. After the scene, she stormed through the swinging waist-high gate separating the kitchen from the dining area, and out the glass doors.

She came back the very next day, requesting her final paycheck. Of course it wasn't yet available. "I want my money," Kim demanded as though destitute. It was the principle. She didn't need the job and wasn't going to put up with anything she didn't like when she was only flipping burgers for fun with her friends.

I didn't need McDonald's for food or shelter, but to continue stacking up social currency—which ushered me into a crowd of kids who wouldn't have noticed me at previous schools. This was a critical development because Kim, Iris, and Kasey transferred to a high school outside Gary for senior year. They thought "Calumet" would look better than "Lew Wallace" on their transcripts when we applied to colleges, as city schools had become shameful. My mother wouldn't let me follow them. (Another brick.) But it only took a couple months for their concerns to be again proven valid.

On October 10, 1997, under Friday night lights, someone shot a schoolmate dead at our homecoming football game. Such an incident is sad on immeasurable levels without context. It's even more sad because she was an innocent bystander, more devastating still because she was six months pregnant. Shot in the head, she stood no chance.

Our impression of high school fun would be forever stained. Sporting events were moved earlier in the day. Some schools declined to visit ours altogether. During the gunman's trial, witnesses alleged he was a member of the Vice Lords gang and had been shooting at rival Gangster Disciples in a crowd of attendees.

I wasn't at the game because every part of Gary seemed dangerous. Shootings like this one also confirmed my mother's point that spending too much time outside the house was dangerous. I only found out what happened the following Monday at school.

Girls were weeping at their lockers and putting up memorial posters that read, "Rest in Peace Kellie." I didn't know her. Yet, I'm able to recall the picture from the posters with precise detail. I see her face as though she were someone familiar. With a short haircut and perfect teeth, she reminded me of the character Kimberly Reese from one of my favorite TV shows, *A Different World*.

This was the year Danny came to Lew Wallace. As a freshman, our mother had let him attend West Side, where all his friends went. He made new friends right away and got closest to Mikey, a short, skinny guy with a serious face who wore his clothes three sizes too big. But I got to see him smile. I got to hear Mikey talk and laugh when he hung out with Danny in our basement later than we were allowed to be out.

I don't know what Mikey did or who he got mixed up with when he wasn't with Danny, but they found him. They covered the side of his little red Ford Escort with bullet holes. The drive-by shooting happened not far from school. Mikey died in the hospital shortly after.

Glen Park was no longer considered a more pleasant suburb of Gary. Kids at other high schools gave Lew Wallace a new nickname, *Murder High*. It was all bad and getting rapidly worse.

"But you're the one who made me stay at this school!" I protested when my mom went on about how dangerous it was and forbade me from attending a sock hop or football game. "I should be at Calumet with Kasey 'nem anyway!"

I was wrecked when I couldn't transfer with my friends but would've been absolutely destroyed if left alone again. Thankfully, I knew more people by then. With my trendy wardrobe and even a nice used car, I'd achieved a respectable peer ranking. Cool-adjacent.

Getting my gray 1994 Buick Skylark with power windows and seats was like strapping a rocket to my popularity. Girls I exchanged casual banter with wanted to hang out. They asked if they could ride along for off-campus lunches. Were some of them using me? Who knows. Who cared? Not me.

I was driving past classmates who were walking to school. I was the one with something not everyone else had but wanted. What I learned was, I could buy my way to worthiness.

Most girls our age went for little stylish cars like Dodge Neons and Ford Probes. Cars like what my new, fourth best friend drove. Timika lived right around the corner from me with her married parents, and I would forever marvel at how effortlessly she loved. She zipped around with her boyfriend in a brand-new Chevy Cavalier. More drawn to luxury than sport, here I was pushing a large family sedan with a front license plate that read, *Supa Dupa Fly*. And you couldn't tell me I wasn't.

Marcus, my new boyfriend, attended West Side but worked at McDonald's. It's where we met. He was the first male after Daddy to tell me, "I love you." His was one of the few verbal declarations of love I had received from anyone in my seventeen years. My mother wrote *Love, Mom* inside birthday cards but didn't say the three-word phrase out loud. Neither did Grandma. Thus, Danny and I didn't say it to one another. I couldn't take it personally. No one said it to anyone.

There's something about hearing the affirmation, watching each word flow from someone's mouth. The more Marcus said it to me, the easier it became to say it back. The more I meant it. We even had a song, "Nothing Even Matters" by Lauryn Hill, featuring D'Angelo. Marcus and I discovered the song separately, but agreed the lyrics perfectly described how we each felt about the other. We played our song on the way to dinner and movies or even just taking a break outside McDonald's sometimes. Sitting in my car, my head resting against his shoulder, we'd gently sway along with the soothing vocals. We decided this would be our wedding song when we got married.

Marcus told me a *real man* should only be soft around his lady. So, I knew he was only this way with me, but didn't know the extent of his alter ego. It wasn't like Eric, where I got to watch him outside the confines of our relationship. Because Marcus went to a different school, I rarely saw how he behaved when I wasn't around. He didn't have a car and never wore anything flashy. I only viewed him as my loving boyfriend who held actual hours-long conversations with me on the phone, kissed me on my forehead, and showed up to my house on Christmas with the huge stereo I'd been coveting. Until one day I got a glimpse into his other life.

We were both sitting on his twin bed when Marcus bent down and slid a shoe box from underneath it. He flipped the top off, pulled a stack of money from the shoe box, and handed me a couple of hundred-dollar bills. "Go get ya hair and nails done." He smiled, said it with pride. He was excited to have the cash to treat his girlfriend to something special.

Before my confused mind could form a question, Marcus told me his friends had robbed our McDonald's. He broke down the entire scheme for me, including how all he did was leave the door unlocked after they closed. "I made sure they did it on a day you weren't there." he tried to reason. "But Kasey was there!" I whined. "She hid inside a box, afraid the robbers might shoot her!"

"Well, I didn't rob the joint," he shrugged. "They were going to do it anyway."

Was this hush money? His or mine? Both? Thoughts swirled around my brain. I could almost see Marcus trying to suck the intended justification back in, sitting on his bed with the open shoe box on his lap, eyes asking me to say something. He put his head down, lifted it a few seconds later, waved his hand and dismissed the entire situation.

"Pfft . . . It's not a big deal, man. Nobody got hurt, man. They weren't gonna shoot your friend. Gone get ya hair and nails did." He ended with a condescending laugh and changed the subject.

I don't know why Marcus didn't lie about where he'd gotten the money, but he should have. He knew me well after more than a year. He knew my family and how I'd been raised. I suppose he thought my love would conquer all. It did not. I couldn't look at him the same.

We were from a place filled with people living below the poverty line who sometimes did disgraceful things to temporarily rise above it. To survive. I understood the temptation, just not the succumbing. I couldn't comprehend ignoring potential consequences.

Danny was also employed at Mickey D's, and Marcus questioned his toughness from shift one. He called me all excited one night, after coercing Danny to stand up for himself and fight a fellow employee who'd said something "disrespectful." He was thrilled to relay how my brother confronted the guy and "whooped his ass." He measured masculinity as many males measure masculinity, in levels of aggression and ability to brawl.

"I was worried about him, man!" he chuckled. "But nah, he's good with me. After tonight I can't mess with him no more. He was throwing haymakers!"

Marcus was a year older than me, set to graduate when the robbery happened. The thug life we might have together flashed before my eyes and I wanted no part of it. I wanted more, starting with getting out of this dreadful town someday, not digging my heels deeper into it.

I thought Marcus needed someone more street savvy who would be fine with delinquent behavior and used this as an excuse to break up with him. He disagreed, thought it was me who kept him in line, from doing worse things.

A few weeks later, there was an article in the newspaper. It said Marcus had snatched an elderly woman's purse. When he told me the whole story, it was the first time I saw him cry. "Martin did that shit, man. I told him not to." His brother snatched the purse. Marcus was with him, and the one police caught. "Do you know how that feels, man? To come in here and have my granny looking at me like I would do something like that?" Shame summoned his tears, and he knew, that was it for me.

Marcus had just left McDonald's. Ill-equipped to act as anyone's savior, I then left him. He brought me roses and stuffed animals. He swore to change and asked me on dates. Never one to let emotions overrule logic, I'd already flipped the switch.

Four years of decent grades earned me a high school diploma. My mother tracked down a surprise guest for my graduation open house. When I came out to greet everyone in the backyard, sitting at one the tables, resting against her cane, brows raised, was Grandmama. Something ignited inside me. I ran over and threw my arms around her neck.

"Grandmama so proud of you," she said and handed me a card. I stood with my hand on her shoulder as we posed for a picture. She looked good, well put together wearing a navy-blue dress, pearl necklace and matching earrings. She also appeared tired. Her low eyes were yellowish red, and she barely smiled for our photo.

Grandmama ate and people watched a bit. Every time I turned to find her, she was watching me, content. She had this glazed look of satisfaction on her face that made me feel proud. Made me happy she was there. She fought through all that ailed her that day, for me.

Unable to move around much though, she didn't stay long. I gave her another hug. "Thank you for coming."

"Bye Grandmama's baby."

My mother helped her up from the table and drove her home.

Not long after, she died. Grandma told me I needed to come to the funeral with her because, "she always tried to do right." Grandmama tried to carve out a place in my world and make room for me in hers.

I wish I would have loved her better, appreciated her

more. While I avoided reminders of Champ, I think she was trying to hold on. She had the pictures and the medals, and then she had me, made in the image of her prodigal son. It hurts not to have your father, but it must also hurt not to have your child. I like to think for a little while I helped soothe Grandmama's aching.

During our entire drive to the funeral, though Grandma didn't mention it, I couldn't help wondering if I might see my father. What would I say to him? I considered whether I should pretend I didn't see him if I did, and release any pressure he might feel to acknowledge me. Forever trying not to be a burden, I thought about what would be easiest for him.

We pulled into the church parking lot. I examined the cars, trying to guess which belonged to Champ. According to Grandmama, he didn't have money. So, I settled on rusting sedans and modest pickup trucks.

Grandma and I sneaked in late and slid into a back pew. She had on one of her tallest, fanciest hats. A small choir sang hymns. Every couple of verses Grandma shouted "Amen!"

There was a photo of Grandmama displayed near a closed casket in front of the choir. Her brown, round face smiled through red lipstick. Champ and I share her chipmunk cheeks. Short hair curled tightly against her forehead. She looked just as I most remembered her. Bubbly. Happy.

When the service was over, Grandma walked me around the church and introduced me as "Mary's granddaughter." The announcement shocked most people. Women placed their hands over their chests, clutched pearls and gasped, "Granddaughter?" Everyone told me I looked just like Champ. "Doesn't she?" They tapped a neighboring funeral-goer on the shoulder and asked for confirmation of the resemblance.

There weren't many people at the service, so making our rounds didn't take long. One of our final stops was with the pastor who delivered the eulogy. He raved about how Grand-mama was a special, God-fearing woman. Grandma nodded in agreement.

I wanted my father to attend but didn't know it until he didn't. Scanning the scantily filled room for his face and listening for someone to offer his whereabouts consumed me. No one mentioned him except in reference to my presence. All my fret-ting proved futile. He didn't show. At least not while I was there.

The result left me somewhat relieved. Relieved I didn't have to face him. Relieved I didn't have to posture with him in front of all the people who'd expect me to behave like his daughter. People who would smash us together and compare the similar-ities of our unfamiliar qualities. Relieved neither of us had to figure out how to handle the other.

But what could be so pressing that would prevent a man with the word "mom" tattooed on his arm from attending his mother's funeral? Especially a mother who sifted through loads of unsavory attributes to highlight the good in her son. Perhaps both she and I were holding on to varying degrees of an illusion portraying who he might have been.

I imagined Champ came into the funeral after Grandma and me. That he'd stood in the back of the church, nestled against a wall. Hiding from the sorrow. Carrying a weight too heavy to drag to the casket. Maybe he said a prayer, asking for forgive-ness or strength. Maybe both. Or neither. He probably would've clenched the crucifix dangling from the gold necklace he wore when I saw him last. That's what someone's son might do at their funeral.

I imagined his eyes found me sitting in one of the pews. That he tried to muster a satisfied smile before making an exit as quiet as his entry. Because he saw me. He saw how bright and beautiful I was, and felt ashamed.

11
Room For Happy Endings

After graduation, my soulmates and I went to separate colleges, in separate cities, chasing our separate dreams. Iris left for Jefferson City, Missouri. Kim and Kasey went two hours away to Indianapolis. I took a break from school and left McDonald's for a better paying telemarketing job while I figured out what to do with myself.

Before leaving for college, Iris connected me with one of her childhood friends. She hoped Shavon and I would hit it off so she wouldn't have to worry about either of us being alone, as we were both inclined to be. It worked despite us not having much at all in common.

Once, on our way to visit Iris, navigating dark, narrow asphalt, a deer darted out in front of my Skylark. By the time I saw it, I'd hit it. The deer stopped and turned toward me; headlights bounced off its eyes glaring through the windshield as though I'd offended it. My foot hovered above the gas pedal, prepared to floor it if the deer made a move, but it galloped across the road and into the other side of the woods.

I arrived at Iris' dorm with a dented hood and broken grill, deer fur stuck between its remaining pieces. She came out, surveyed the sight, and erupted into laughter. I laughed too. We laughed together, leaning on the smashed hood under a streetlight, speculating about how the deer might gather its homies and come after me. I never used to find the humor in hardship. But for those few moments, I lost all concern for how I would pay to fix the damage.

Shavon had her father. She also had a toddler, a cute little redhead who amused herself by throwing stuffed animals Shavon's way until she got bored.

I spent my gap year partying and getting high with Shavon when I wasn't getting cursed out and hung up on by those I solicited at my telemarketing gig. We sometimes sat in her bedroom and drank forty-ounce bottles of Old English beer and the cheapest wine we could find, Mad Dog 20/20 or Boone's Farm, until we threw up. Well, until I threw up, the lightweight of every crew. Neither of us yet twenty-one, a relative of hers would score the booze for us if we couldn't charm whomever was working the liquor store counter. We chain-smoked Newports, the cool rush of menthol to our heads providing a slight buzz. When wanting a stronger high, we smoked weed. It wasn't hard to come by since most of our acquaintances sold marijuana or knew someone who did.

It was always the two of us, and often her two high-school-aged nieces. Though both were younger than me, their household was much looser. They were already doing all the reckless teenage stuff I was just getting into.

We piled into my car in the middle of one night and passed a blunt around while I drove us somewhere blasting Lil' Kim. One of the nieces leaned forward in slow motion from the back seat and said something, syllable-by-syllable. Or at least my inebriated brain processed the sentence that way. "Ca-mey . . . you . . . on . . . the . . . wrong . . . side . . . of . . . the . . . road . . ."

"Huh?" I didn't grasp what she was trying to articulate until headlights obscured my vision. "Oh shit!" I swerved over to the proper lane. Once everyone's insides settled, we laughed like idiots and went back to Shavon's apartment where we belonged.

We walked through the front door, loud and giggly, reeking of weed. Shavon's father, watching TV from his living room La-Z-Boy, was wearing a navy-blue robe and drinking a can of Old Style. He gave us a stern look but didn't say anything.

"Quiet down in there!" her father sometimes yelled if we got too boisterous. "Shut up Daddy!" Shavon yelled back. My mouth dropped when I first witnessed the exchange. I didn't have a father but, based on my upbringing, felt confident that if I'd had one, he'd have knocked my teeth out for such sassiness. Most amazing to me was that she talked to her dad this way and he still loved her.

On weekends, we partied in public. We slid on our boot-cut jeans and baby doll t-shirts with a pair of Nike Air Max and drove to the same club in Chicago every other Saturday because they didn't card anyone. Inside, many of the men were very much grown. Some looked to be pushing forty with balding heads and graying beards. They grabbed our waists and danced on our butts, and we let them. Me, Shavon, and the nieces faced one another. We laughed and held each other's hands in the air as men reminiscent of our uncles pulsated behind us. The room was packed with people, shoulder to shoulder. It would've been difficult to stop them if we tried. If we cared.

We filed out of the club sometimes close to two a.m. and let the night chill whisk over the thin layer of sweat covering our foreheads. It was the best part of the evening, this release from stuffiness into the flow of fresh, cool air. Even in winter, with snow stacked on the sidewalks, we partied at our favorite club. Everyone was drunk. Walking back to my car once, an intoxicated party-goer backed out of his parking space without checking to see if there were people behind him. He bumped into Shavon, sending her sliding sideways, knees bent across the ice-covered parking lot.

"Oh my God!" I screamed. "Are you okay?" She was doubled over in a low squat position but still on her feet, giggling. "I'm fine! But wait. I just got hit by a car, dude!" Wasted from weed and alcohol, and possibly a couple of her anxiety pills, it took Shavon a minute to realize what had happened.

After seeing she was indeed not hurt, we both fell into frenzied laughter. Unbelievable. She was hit by a car, as a pedestrian, and didn't hit the pavement.

The driver of the vehicle stopped after impact. He turned to look at us with a straight face. No horror, no shock, didn't roll his window down to ask if my friend was okay. "You hit me!" she yelled, walking toward his window. He grimaced, finished reversing, and spun his tires out into the street.

My history with Shavon wasn't all wild and irresponsible. With aging parents and a daughter to take care of, she was also very nurturing. When I stayed the night she made us breakfast in the morning. She washed the clothes I'd worn over without my asking. She took me to get my nails done when I was broke, and nursed my belly back to health when it was overwhelmed by cheap liquor.

Still, much of our time together produced self-imposed chaos. Our friendship lasted almost my entire first year out of high school, until it became obvious we not only didn't have enough in common to sustain the relationship but it also wasn't good for me. Almost killed us on more than one occasion.

This was the closest I had ever come to losing myself. I think I needed this phase to let my hair down and be free. I needed to make mistakes and have it turn out okay. Still, it made me ask, *Who am I?*

I'd spent the past year being someone in stark contrast to who I'd been my entire life, and all I'd discovered was that I could be anyone. So, I turned to my always easier-to-answer question: What am I good at?

Church. Speeches. Spelling bees. School. I recalled the reverence of my public speaking and how I shied more often from intimate gatherings than I did from crowds. Maybe there was something there for which Grandma had groomed me.

I thought about how my mother used to scold me for staying up past my bedtime, for how reading with nothing but a nightlight would ruin my eyes. *That book will be there tomorrow.* Yes, but will the escape? I remembered the saving grace of stories and was compelled to study television production at Columbia College in Chicago.

When my mom and I went to the campus open house, faculty solicited volunteers to run through a mock newscast. I raised my hand and took a swing at hosting the show. They directed me atop a stool positioned in front of a camera. There was a teleprompter. "Just read what comes up on the screen," someone said. "Action!"

A red "On Air" light popped on in the studio and words scrolled up the display. I read it all in one take, impeccably. The faculty, other parents, and students clapped when I finished. They said I was a natural and seemed relaxed, like I'd been on TV before. My mother smiled. She looked proud as people raved to her about my performance. Proud like she did when folks complimented my outfit on Easter Sunday. And as much as I resisted caring, her approval still pleased the kid inside me.

I was sold. This. Is. What. I. Do. The formula worked here. We got me enrolled for the upcoming fall semester.

———

As a girl, I was gifted numerous diaries and notebooks, all of which were left forgotten after a few entries. "Put your feelings in here," the gifters would tell me. But exploring those hidden parts and the idea of expressing what I found made me uneasy. I couldn't write about my actual life. Film school offered another way to get some of the benefits of journaling.

In class, we put together storyboards and scripted ideas for TV shows. All my stories were gratuitously sad. I storyboarded a mother sitting by the bedside of her terminally ill kid, having tender conversations about love and admiration. Then when the kid died, the mother didn't want to go on. Her child was her reason for rising in the mornings. I wrote characters who were snake bitten and justifiably self-loathing. One was let go from his job, then got into a car accident and came home to find his house on fire. His dog got out but ran away.

I left no room for happy endings. My characters experienced relentless suffering until the story was just . . . over. No silver lining. No lesson except *life is pain.*

It was easier to write about emotions when I fictionalized them. *This is how Lisa feels.* I avoided composing plots even remotely resembling my life. I didn't believe any of my narratives were about me, though all probably were in some manner. Whether the mom was telling her kid things I wished my parents had told me, or a girl lost everything she loved, there were pieces of me in there. The stories weren't mine, but the underlying tone was.

The instructor had to be concerned, possibly even disturbed, while consuming my buffet of pain porn. But I got good grades because art is subjective. If one follows the rules of the assignment, it can't be wrong just because someone doesn't like the content.

I felt more engaged in school than I had since elementary. Attending Columbia was everything I imagined. We produced internal talk shows, filmed newscasts, and watched popular TV sitcoms or dramas as homework. Learning was fun. But after three semesters of hour-long train rides to and from my northwest Indiana home, and mile-long treks through rain, snow, and freezing temperatures, the WNBA happened, and I started to rethink what I really wanted.

It didn't help that my out-of-state tuition was expensive. I was taking out massive student loans just to attend Columbia part-time. Plus, I held doubts about the likelihood of breaking into television production as a sustainable career after learning the percentage of graduates who did so was minuscule. As much as I loved the field, turning it into something significant seemed unlikely.

Oddly, I thought my chances at becoming one of less than a hundred women in the WNBA were greater.

Watching Sheryl Swoopes, Tina Thompson, Cynthia Cooper and the Houston Comets dynasty awakened my YWCA middle school passion. Now I saw a place it could take me and wanted to go there. Problem was, my arts-focused institution didn't have any athletic programs.

I'm going to the WNBA. I was convinced. Growing up delivering on the expectation of perfection gave me confidence in my ability, though not in my personhood. But I believed if I did the work, I could achieve anything I wanted. And I wanted this more than I wanted to work in television. I left my prestigious Chicago film school and enrolled at a local university with a basketball team I could join.

The Purdue Calumet coach was a former military man who still looked the part. He was bald and pale, with no facial hair, and missing half an index finger. The way he barked out commands, you'd swear we were on a battlefield. "Move! Stop! Next! Get over here! You're done!" Coach Smith didn't engage in much conversation or explanation.

I made the team on my second attempt. The first try, I was absurdly out of shape. People look at you when you're skinny and assume you're healthy or must exercise. I wasn't and didn't. For a while there, breathing during and after workouts became such a challenge, I thought I might have asthma. I bought an over-the-counter inhaler, but pumping it into my mouth after attempting a brisk jog did nothing. It did not soothe the burning in my chest or open what were surely my collapsed lungs, because I didn't have asthma.

Coach broke the news while we were still doing preseason conditioning drills. After the other girls lapped me for the last time during the eight-minute-mile we were supposed to run, he'd seen enough. I was strolling. Hands on my hips and panting, I had the audacity to display such a pitiful performance as a hopeful walk-on. You have all these recruited girls with assured roster spots busting their butts to run a mile, and then me. Someone uninvited. Someone supposedly trying to earn a spot, dogging it. Wasn't a good look.

I sped up a bit and bounced across the finish line. Coach was there waiting. "We're going to have to cut you," he said with a crooked smile, as though the discussion made him uncomfortable. My face had the further audacity to display a look of disbelief. "Can you just give me one more chance?" He looked down at the ground, over to the assistant coach who was also a player's father, then back up at me. "What I'm saying is, no."

I thought my youth summer league experience, plus playing pickup games with my brother and cousin in the driveway (giving them buckets, I might add) prepared me to play at the collegiate level. I was furious Coach Smith cut me before we'd even gotten to touch a ball. He made the decision based on what he saw on the track and during exercise routines. I mean, we're talking about *conditioning*. Not a *game*. Not the game I played on cracked concrete between oil spills as the sun set. We're talking about conditioning.

My anger gave way to disappointment and hurt, which I channeled into something I hadn't felt before, determination. I picked myself up and decided I was going to make Purdue Calumet's team. I'd sacrificed too much not to. I couldn't give up one dream only to fail at its replacement. The thought of leaving film school behind for naught was unbearable.

I gave every free moment of my post-cut summer to running, lifting weights, watching instructional videos, shooting in the driveway, and learning about the game. When fall sports convened, I was there with the women's basketball team. I worked harder than I had for anything ever, and it paid off. I was the one lapping people during our eight-minute-mile and among the first to cross the finish line. I was the one waiting, smiling, and encouraging as others sucked air and collapsed over their knees. I was the one clapping while reaffirming "Good job" and "You can do it!" Felt damn good too.

Despite all my off-season training, I remained barely one hundred pounds. Lifting weights was still a challenge, but the other girls helped me. They'd place a hand under the bar while I benched pressed, just enough to offer a gentle added lift when I struggled to push the weight all the way up. They'd switch spots with me and pretend I'd completed a set of twelve reps when I stalled out at ten.

My greatest void was where a male parental figure might be, but I was always saved by females. First my high school friends. Now my teammates.

Everyone else on the team held guaranteed scholarships. I posed little threat to their playing time. They wanted me to make it, which made me want to make it more and go harder. It's the camaraderie of which every athlete reminisces. Bonds forged in the fire of a shared goal are unmatched. Together, we secured my roster spot.

My favorite teammates were from central Illinois and shared an apartment together near the school. We hung out at their place most. One of them, Krystal, had a ferret, a gift from her dad meant to keep her company. I wasn't an animal person, and uncommon household pets like ferrets especially weirded me out. Krystal would confine her ferret to a different room when I came over. Isolation worked until the weasel discovered his body could flatten itself enough to slither below the door.

It was a thoughtful gift, the ferret. Though she had a room-mate and eleven teammates, her dad wanted her to have something to care for and cuddle. Though I wasn't a fan of the pet, the sentiment made me smile. It was interesting to me how others saw separation from family as a difficult circumstance.

Krystal's dad also came up and installed a security bar inside the front door to her apartment. The school and her place were in Hammond, not Gary, but close enough to cause concern. I think her dad would've been just as involved no matter where his daughter lived. He worried about her safety with him a couple of hours away. She promised to secure the door every night, mostly to help calm his anxious mind.

Sometimes she got annoyed. It was overwhelmed annoy-ance. Like *I appreciate your concern, but it's a tad too much.* Still, she assembled the bar every night like her father asked. She took in the ferret like he hoped. She let him protect his little girl.

I thought it was excessive. Thought he called too much. But maybe I only thought that because I didn't know what love looked like.

He also got her a nice purple coupe to drive around town. We went for rides to White Castle and other local food spots while Krystal played the latest mix CD she'd created. Her play-lists were always the most random, least orchestrated collections of songs. There'd be hardcore hip-hop followed by 90s R&B or a lovesick ballad. DMX followed by Shania Twain followed by NSYNC followed by Green Day followed by Celine Dion followed by Snoop Dogg. It was all over the place.

Normally, you made mix CDs to set a specific mood, You had one with slow songs you'd play when setting a romantic atmosphere with another person, or when alone and dreaming of having a person. You had a CD with high energy songs to get you going. Maybe you had a disc with all sad songs or complete gangster rap. Point is, the arrangements were usually consistent. Not my buddy's though. She threw together her latest favorite tunes in no particular order and jammed out. She introduced me to artists I'd never heard and genres I'd never considered, like alternative. For a while, groups like Coldplay, The Fray, and Staind played heaviest in my rotation. It was the passion of the music that drew me in. The perpetual agony. The way they expressed feelings for which I couldn't find words.

A Staind song came up in her track sequence one day, "Zoe Jane." I immediately knew it was a love song, the beauty of the opening lyrics giving it away.

How sweet. I listened as my friend sang along while a guitar wept in the background. The final line of the chorus surprised me. Aaron Lewis wasn't professing the type of adoration I'd imagined. He said he'd always love her, "the way that a father should love his daughter."

"Sweet Zoeeee Jaaane," Lewis goes on to drawl. He adored his daughter enough to arrange such a stirring melody? I stared out the window as Krystal continued gripping her purple steering wheel cover, belting out every word reminiscent of sentiments I'd grown certain her father held for her. Surely "Zoe Jane" wasn't the most beautiful thing I'd ever heard, but on that day it felt like it, and sometimes still does. Sometimes, when I think I'm past idolizing the daddy-daughter dynamic, I'm not.

I adored my teammate because of how she expanded my world. The way she saw me as I might one day see myself, as a whole person she could tell her secrets to and with whom she could be vulnerable. She wasn't afraid to talk about anything—accepting herself and others as they were.

Her grandmother died during the season. I came to offer comfort, anticipating a person more somber than who I found. She was smiling between the moments she shed a tear or two.

The explanation for her lack of distress stayed with me long after. "I didn't really know her," she said. "I mean, I knew her as the role she played in my life, but not as a person." I understood infinitely what she meant and said no more. There was caution in her voice as she made the statement. The hesitancy said "I know I'm probably not supposed to say this but . . . " I got it. I related to the words as soon as they left her mouth.

I understood people expecting specific reactions out of you. I knew what it meant to feel a bit callous when family to you seemed but a word, a label, a bloodline descriptor untethered from emotion. She was sad her dad lost his mom. Her tears were for him.

I sprawled my body across her living room futon many nights. Laughing. Talking. Being. Until darkness rolled into daylight.

The next season I earned a modest partial basketball scholarship that my tuition costs all but swallowed. The other girls had full rides and most came from well-to-do families who gave them money and covered expenses they couldn't cover themselves. Most of them didn't rely on student loans and Pell grants, like me. Yet, here I was practicing and playing and hanging out at teammates' apartments as though these were my only concerns. As though I were one of them. For a while, it felt like I might be. I lived in their lives. I shoved my feet into their shoes and meandered about. Practicing, playing, hanging became my routine. I loved every carefree minute of it—including the minutes I rode the bench and got yelled at by Coach. Even the seconds he thrust me into the deepest depths of public humiliation.

I didn't know how to check-in to a game. I was lost during the most basic play calls and drills because I hadn't played organized basketball since grade school. Again, the game moved fast, just like in the YWCA league. Except I was in college and people expected me to know better. Plus, I was afraid to make a mistake, which is kryptonite to most athletes. You have to act instinctively. Coach would lose it at my cluelessness and hesitancy.

What made those moments easier to endure were pats on the back and encouragement from my teammates. They held me. Shielded me. They pulled me close when I would've otherwise withdrawn.

When I made the team only to be cut again at the start of my second season, I was decimated. I stayed in the gym, the hardest working member of the team. How could Coach do this to me? "You can keep the scholarship," he said. I emptied my locker into a duffel bag and ran to my car, praying I wouldn't see Krystal or any of the other girls with whom I'd grown inseparable. Seeing their faces I was certain would twist the knife in my chest.

Once home, my levees broke. I rushed into my room, shut the door, and bawled into a pillow so hard it only slightly muffled the sound. "What's wrong?" my mother kept asking through the locked door.

"It must be about basketball," I heard Danny say. "She only gets this upset over basketball."

The next day my stepfather, who worked at a small college, told me he'd talked to the coach of their women's basketball team. I was invited to join without even trying out. My floundering spirit, still learning it had wings, accepted.

———

At the new school there was a girl who hung around the team. Every day she rolled into the gym in her wheelchair and was often already there when I arrived. She had long black hair draped over the front of her shoulders and wore glasses. With a broad smile, she sat and watched our practices, cheering everyone on, or sometimes assisting with tasks like keeping score and distributing towels. She didn't talk much otherwise. I didn't learn her name right away, but her consistent presence was unmissable and the way she helped and encouraged us, appreciated.

During our first game, I saw her wearing a cheerleading uniform with the rest of the squad on the baseline. Again, always smiling, she shook pom poms in front of, next to, and above her head with supreme enthusiasm. She shouted loudest of everyone from start to finish, win or lose.

Whether we sucked or sucked less, she treated us like the '96 Chicago Bulls, like victors of record-setting proportion. She slapped each of our hands after the contest, telling us, "Good game," even if it wasn't. If our on-court performance was undeniably horrid, as it often was, the joy it brought her remained apparent. Something we took for granted, being an athlete, she treated like an accomplishment worthy of rockstar treatment.

She didn't seem concerned with developing friendships, only with staying close to us as a unit, to the game. I supposed she must have loved basketball like me, and through us, she played vicariously.

My stepsister came into town for a few days. When she found out I'd joined the basketball team at her father's college, she asked if I'd seen her, the cheerleader in a wheelchair. They grew up in the same neighborhood and remained close friends after my stepsister moved to Terre Haute. She told me her friend wasn't born disabled. She was in an accident when they were kids and sustained the trajectory-altering injuries.

Her name is Adrienne.

I wish to say her name because I haven't said it before. Because I wish for her not to be defined as the girl in the wheelchair when, to our team and her loved ones, she was more.

Had Adrienne not been in an accident, would she be on the court with me? Seeing how we shared a passion for the game, might she have been my teammate? What might we have been if unforgiving fate had seen fit to also leave her dreams untouched?

It's why she connected to the game more intently than your average fan or cheerleader, I thought. At one point, she could see herself playing basketball, and possibly did. Adrienne had a different life once.

What my stepsister said next was most jolting. She'd discovered her friend and I have the same father.

Adrienne was my biological sister. We were less than a year apart in age.

How odd it was to share space with someone just about every day with no idea of such close relation. This wasn't a long-lost cousin, but a sibling. I'd gone more than twenty years believing I only had a brother. Now I had a sister. It made me consider how many more of Champ's children might exist out there, severed from family ties.

I don't know if my biological sister discovered who I was and told my stepsister or if my stepsister connected the dots and delivered the same news to Adrienne she'd dropped on me. Either way, the disclosure didn't change anything for either of us. We both continued to come in and do what we'd come to do without unusual acknowledgment of the other.

Perhaps the early introduction to detachment, a result of withstanding the same absent father, conditioned us to take this approach. Reaching for one another struck us as odder than pretending there was no reason to do so. Did she feel what I felt?

Had lovelessness also consumed the parts of her not buried beneath sorrow? I didn't see any evidence. Maybe it was a facade, but Adrienne came across as entirely alive. She was happy and smiling and moved with purpose when I saw her. She had something I did not, joy, at least on the outside. She had a lightness while I struggled to hold the weight accompanying every second of every day. We each watched the other do things we were unable to do, and I questioned which of us was actually most free.

Adrienne and I carried on holding a secret of which we both knew the other was aware. We did it without so much as a knowing smirk in the other's direction. She didn't talk to me. I didn't talk to her, even though our silence felt peculiar, intentional now, like avoidance.

She'd scream the other girls' names when they did something on the court. "Good job Rachel! Let's go Jenny!" But not mine. Granted, I was new to the team, not as familiar to her as the other girls. But we barely looked at each other after learning the secret. There was an elephant in the room neither of us seemed ready or willing to acknowledge.

Shortly after, and for unrelated reasons, I left to join the basketball team at a rival university and never saw Adrienne again.

Still, I could admit to myself the unlikely coincidence of she and I both loving basketball. Of us finding our way to the same school, the same basketball team. Even in the small region of Gary and its surrounding areas, a perfect storm had to occur: my mother remarrying, me getting cut from my original team, my stepfather getting a job at the college and remaining there into my college years, Adrienne enrolling at the same school at the same time, becoming a cheerleader. All of it led us to crash into one another.

I hate that he did that to us, Champ. Made connection feel bizarre. Made us reluctant to acknowledge we were sisters. Because as much as she was to our team and her loved ones, she could've been more to me, too.

12

Smoking Deal

The car salesman was speaking through a neatly trimmed handlebar mustache. "I don't see a lot of young ladies come through by themselves. You didn't have anyone who knows about cars to come with you?" By "anyone," he meant a father, a brother, a man.

"Nah," I said. "I saw an ad in the paper for this car and liked it."

"Where do you go to school?" He changed the subject.

I did many things he probably didn't see young ladies doing by themselves—car shopping, minor vehicle repairs, taking long road trips. I was fully cemented in radical independence. Fully committed to shunning help that, without the assurance of love, felt like pity.

His line of questioning didn't offend me. I got these inquiries often, and those who asked weren't entirely off base or chauvinistic. Their concerns were likely a significant factor in how I ended up with this salesman, looking to purchase a ten-year-old Cadillac Eldorado with 50,000 miles.

Before this, I "qualified" for a brand-new gold Dodge Stratus from one of those seedy neighborhood dealerships. You know the ones situated in poor neighborhoods with phrases like "Smoking Deal" painted neon green on the windshields of cars. Alone always and without guidance, I jumped at the $500 monthly payments I wrongly convinced myself I could afford. This was $300 more than I'd been paying for the Skylark I'd traded in before quitting my full-time job to play basketball. Scraping up the difference while a student-athlete living on about $12,000 a year bordered on impossible. Worse, the Stratus was brand new trash, not worth anything near its price tag.

Shortly after driving it off the lot, I could tell there was something wrong with the transmission. The entire car jerked when downshifting gears. It would thrust forward a bit with a loud "boom!" when coming to a complete stop.

I took the Stratus into the dealership for service several times. Several times I left with the issue unresolved. A Lemon-Law attorney got me out of the deal.

With a few thousand dollars from my financial aid refund check, I replaced the Stratus with a used blue Chevy Lumina. It broke down a year later, a few weeks before I showed up to purchase this Cadillac with my next refund check. It was sweet, pearl-white with tan leather seats, whitewall tires, and all-electric everything.

"Wanna take it for a spin?" Sales Guy asked. He ran inside the dealership to grab a license plate.

Waiting in the car alone, I rubbed my hand across the soft leather seats and gripped the smooth steering wheel. I could see myself driving it already. Even if Sales Guy had told me the truth when he returned, it might not have swayed me.

I squealed about how the Eldorado must be in great condition since it's been driven so little during its ten years on the road. "Yeah, yeah," he responded as we sat in the car testing all its bells and whistles. "I'm not sure how many owners the car has had. I'll have to check. But yeah, you don't see low miles on older vehicles."

He propped the license plate up inside the rear window. "Alright young lady, let's go!" We only drove the Cadillac a mile or two. Of course, it was fine. The stereo worked. The V8 engine was quiet. It was like cruising atop a cloud. Our drive sealed the deal.

Across the desk, as I filled out the purchasing paperwork, Sales Guy looked uneasy with the half-smile I'd seen before. The *awww* smile. In my head, I rolled my eyes. *I've been a big girl a long time, sir. Please don't feel sorry for me* is what I wanted to say. I signed my name on every necessary line and handed over a cashier's check.

When the deal was done, however, and the salesman's bosses came over, his demeanor changed. "Congratulations young lady!" he exclaimed, dangling a set of keys in the air. "You just bought yourself a gorgeous 1994 Cadillac Eldorado!" He handed the keys over to me while all the guys in khakis and polo shirts applauded.

Sixty days later, I left the Cadillac at CarMax after accepting a $1,600 offer to buy the old luxury vehicle now burning white smoke and running hot in the parking lot. Its analog odometer wasn't displaying abnormally low mileage but had rolled over after hitting its max. No one could tell me how many times this had happened.

Solo at CarMax, I had no idea if they offered me a fair price. But it seemed acceptable considering the vehicle was undriveable. I thought they were doing me a favor by taking it off my hands.

Blowing my refund checks on used cars became a pattern. At least next time, I took the hinted advice of Sales Guy and brought my stepdad with me.

Richard had been to the automobile auction in Illinois. He knew how to get there and get in, but we didn't arrive early enough to view many cars in advance. Everyone was already gathering in the auction space, which meant I had to make my selection mostly sight unseen.

Auction workers drove vehicles, freshly sprayed with water, through the warehouse, stopping for a few minutes in front of spectators who offered bids. Most of the wet cars looked great on the outside. Nice and shiny.

While vehicles were driven down the auction block, an auctioneer announced each make and model. He raved about how beautiful the cars were and threw in little anecdotes depending on the style. "Perfect for road trips with the family, folks." Or, "If you want to turn heads, take a look at this pretty little thing." After his intro, he flew into the fast-talking bidding process.

"Can I get five hundred dollars? You got five hundred dollars I got five hundred dollars in the corner can I get seven hundred dollars? Seven hundred seven hundred seven hundred I got seven hundred can I get a thousand? A thousand. Can I get fifteen hundred, fifteen hundred. Can I get two thousand? Two thousand two thousand two thousand? Fifteen hundred dollars . . . going once . . . going twice . . . sold to number thirty-seven!"

An emerald-green Buick Regal was the first car driven through for which I offered a winning bid, though I'd lifted my auction paddle for just about everything except minivans and SUVs. The fast paced pressured you to quickly raise your paddle for fear of missing out.

"That one right thurr looks good, daughter," Richard said. "Buicks are good cars. Last a loooong time."

Water running down the Regal made its green look especially rich. A driver steered it through the auction space at about five miles per hour and braked for a couple of minutes until the auctioneer yelled "Sold!" Once claimed, the driver sped to the other end and out of the warehouse.

I went to claim my prize and opened the car door to a horrific scene. It was *filthy*. Not just regular unkemptness with crumbs in the seats and dirt on the floor. Every *inch* of the Buick's interior was covered in layers of black soot. The previous owner must've worked in one of the steel mills. I didn't even want to touch the steering wheel but had to drive the car home as it was. My sleeves got dirty from the arm rest. My hands felt grimy. The back of my shirt stuck to the seat when I tried to get out.

First thing the next morning I dropped the Buick off at an auto detailer. It took them the entire workday to get it clean. Once they did, I discovered the interior was beige. It was beautiful, soft and plushy.

Maybe I had been taken advantage of all those times I went to purchase cars clueless and alone. Because Richard was right. I drove my Regal for years without a single mechanical issue. I drove it to Memphis the summer after college graduation and the end of my modest collegiate basketball run.

With the last of my financial aid money, I went to play for a semi-pro basketball league in Memphis. I moved in with Aunt Niecy for a stint after all, years following my initial attempt. She loved the same as I remembered. Warm. Affectionate. She referred to me as "babe" and "sweetie" even at age twenty-four, and I felt twelve again.

Summer ended along with our season. A couple girls got called up to play in a pro basketball league overseas. Neither of them was me.

Before hitting the road back to Indiana, I picked up my baby niece, Mecca, from her mother's house. Danny had lived in Memphis for a spell, long enough to have a child with his ex-girlfriend. She agreed to let their almost one-year-old daughter spend a few months with my mother and me.

Mecca was an easy travel partner. I strapped her into a car seat where she slept most of the drive and didn't cry one time. Every few hours I stopped to change her diaper, pour more apple juice into her bottle, or get french fries for her to nibble on. That was enough to keep her happy. She bobbed her little round head to my music and smiled, displaying the two teeth protruding from her gums when I glanced back at her through the rearview mirror.

When we got home, Richard and my mom had put a crib in the spare bedroom right next to mine. It belonged to Mecca now. Her every whimper would penetrate my walls.

I found this tiny human astonishing. The way she stretched her arms toward me like she knew I would lift her up. How she cried from her crib in the middle of the night, as though confident one of us would come. I couldn't picture myself ever as sure those around me would satisfy my needs, though I'm certain I was, as the beauty of infancy is innocence. You cry and trust and reach for people instinctually. You don't know any better. Only contrasting experience can teach you otherwise.

Mecca had cheeks so chubby my mother took her to audition for the next local Gerber baby. She put her in a fancy dress, cute little hat, and patent leather shoes when she could barely walk. My mother held Mecca's chunky arms above her head and helped her take tiny steps across the stage. She giggled and drooled, and at one point moved her little legs as though she were trying to take off running. The judges chose Mecca as a finalist. She returned for the next round and brought home a trophy.

When Mecca cried, I ran to her. She'd drop the full weight of her head against my chest or shoulder, and I'd melt. Sometimes she tossed her head side-to-side, trying to get comfy. I worried she might see through my amateur fumblings and know I hadn't held anyone before.

I'd take her to lie with me and gently rub her back until she was again sound asleep. I kissed her cheeks and clutched her tight. The impulse to nurture startled me in the most marvelous manner. I stepped into a different light, the one in which my niece saw me.

When Mecca wrapped her arms around my neck and felt safe enough to collapse, I decided she must always feel this way. She must always know I'm here. Her innocence would dissipate over the years, but I didn't want the certainty that at least one person would always show up for her to fade along with it.

Mecca's parents had her when they were young. Danny was fresh into his twenties and her mother wasn't much older. They were still navigating the financial, cerebral, and psychological paths from youth to full-fledged adulthood when suddenly charged with caring for a child.

It seemed Danny and I were moving in opposite directions. While I was learning to pull a life together that brought me some semblance of peace, inner and outer turmoil was overtaking him. This is all speculation, but surely friends dying, complicated relationships with parents, and being out in the world with not much wisdom on how to navigate it inevitably began weighing on him.

Danny started drinking more and coming around less. Alcohol transformed him into a person I no longer recognized. Whoever made an occasional appearance didn't behave like my brother. Not the sweet, meek, funny one I knew. There were flashes. But overall, this one was empty-eyed and angry. Venomous, his remarks turned senseless and jagged. Like a spoon that cuts with the precision of a knife, you didn't expect or understand it—but his words sliced through you just the same.

Mecca gained a younger brother and sister thanks to Danny. Yet, she was the only one of the bunch who didn't have a consistently present parent. She stayed with my mother the first several years of her life. She went to live with Danny and his wife for a little while and came back. She returned to Memphis with her mom for a bit, and came back. She stayed with Danny and his post-divorce girlfriend at a point, but Mecca living with my mother for a few months turned into almost forever.

This is why I do any and everything I can for her. It's why I've treated her like my child. Because she's someone's child. Someone once close to me. Danny isn't quite Champ but, and I say this with love, he isn't far off.

I still remember the oversized agony of a tiny broken heart and don't want this for Mecca. I don't want her to be like me. Not in this way. She can have my ambition, my discipline, and maybe my independence. She cannot have my melancholy.

I wish for her an embarrassment of adoring riches. I want her to know love and warmth. To give of herself freely in the presence of those with pure intentions. I want her independence to serve as a platform, not a shield.

13
At My Best

A letter arrived at my mother's house. In my mother's name. It was from Champ. The letter was written to both of us, though I didn't read a word. My mother took it into the privacy of her bedroom. A few minutes later she emerged and relayed the information she thought I should know.

In the note, Champ detailed the vastness of his transgressions. He acknowledged the harm caused by his negligence and ignorance. He laid it all out in the process of apologizing. To my knowledge, it was his first confession. His only admission of having done anything for which to be contrite. Eighteen years after leaving me in front of a window, something compelled him to reach into his past and carry it to the present.

I don't know how he got our address. We were living in our third house since I'd seen him last. An educated guess points to Grandma having a hand in the matter. She still lived in the same house he and his girlfriend used to drive past and pause in front of to torment my mother.

Grandma, for all her sternness, remained in favor of forgiving those who trespass against us. She took a no-nonsense approach with family, but was kind and incredibly sensitive to the needs of others. I never knew her to hold a grudge. She relished bringing people together. It's why she baked huge batches of her rolls to serve after church or invited members for dinner. It's why she made me spend time with Grandmama and didn't scold Champ's dad when he showed up drunk outside her house. She had to have been the one who supplied Champ with our address and his opportunity at redemption.

Or wait, maybe it was Grandmama. She was here for my high school graduation party. Champ didn't attend her funeral but that doesn't mean they hadn't talked.

However he got the address, we got the letter. Champ apologized for refusing to claim me as his own. He expressed regret for torturing my mother. He apologized for relinquishing his legal parental rights, allowing another man to attach his last name to my first and take me as his daughter. He expressed remorse for his overall disinterest in my existence. It was from all sins he wished to be cleansed.

The answer to my question of "Why now?" made its way into the letter. It had to. The answer was part of the process.

Champ crafted his message while in an Alcoholics Anonymous program. I was one of his steps. My mother was one of his steps. We were part of his orchestrated journey toward making amends.

I tried to decide if circumstances made his attempt and apology less sincere. Was he truly sorry or did he think he *should* be sorry? Was the apology delivered under duress?

In the letter, Champ left his number and asked us to call him. My mother lifted the cordless phone from its place on the kitchen wall before we returned to our separate bedrooms. She had her own things to discuss and axes to grind.

At least fifteen minutes passed before my mother appeared in my doorway. She had the phone tucked behind her the way you did when you didn't want the person on the other end to hear what you were saying. Leaning into my cracked bedroom door, she whispered.

"Do you want to talk to him?"

"Who?" I don't know why I asked. Short memory, selective memory, or my dedication to indifference took control.

"Your dad. He's on the phone and said he wants to talk to you." She told me he reiterated how sorry he was for everything he'd done to hurt us, and how he was trying to become a better person.

"No," I responded without giving it much thought. "Tell him I forgive him. I'm not mad at him. But I just don't want to talk."

"Okay." She returned the phone to her ear as she walked away.

I carried on watching TV, not the least bit curious about what was being said—or what might have been said if I'd taken the phone. I did hope Champ got some comfort from the knowledge of my forgiveness. I was too exhausted to be angry and too far removed from caring. I held no ill will. I'd just gone so long without him, I didn't see a place or reason for his presence in my life. *Because he's my father* didn't suffice.

I thought about an episode of *The Fresh Prince of Bel-Air*, "Papa's Got a Brand New Excuse," in which Will Smith's character is stood up by his father, again, this time as an adult. At the end of the episode Will realizes his father isn't going to show up as promised. Though visibly hurt and full of raging disappointment, he ran down a list of all his accomplishments, all he'd done and would do without his father. There's a long pause after Will delivers a defiantly pained monologue detailing the greatness of his fatherless life. Very much a grown man, he loses an obvious battle to hold back tears because his daddy didn't come for him. Then he breaks down. He says what his heart wanted to say while his pride went on a rampage.

"How come he don't want me, man?"

My stomach caves into itself at that exact line. Such a simple, innocent question for which there is no answer suitable enough to satisfy any of us fatherless children. Not even when we become adults.

I thought about my own list of achievements and all I'd accomplished in Champ's absence. I went through my own version of Will's lines, many of which were similar.

Got through my first date without him.
Learned how to drive without him.
Made the basketball team without him.
Had twenty-six great birthdays without him.
He never even sent me a damn card!
I ain't need him then and I don't need him now.

I'd learned to live without him. Where Will is distraught, trying to soothe himself with a pep talk, I'm dismissive. Proud. Borderline arrogant. Yet, watching that iconic *Fresh Prince* scene always guts me.

The biggest difference between Will's character and me is, he still believed. He allowed himself to believe again in the father who abandoned him all those years ago. Because he believed, he could be broken, again. In opening himself up to elation and anticipation, he had to open himself up to pain—and as pain tends to do, it found him. I don't know if I can take it finding me.

I've developed a dismissive-avoidant attachment style, is what psychologists would say. I exhibit all the markers: believing you don't need anyone else in your life; feeling a strong sense of

Heavy is the head that wears disenchantment. I adore being a person who might allow someone to love her and imagines herself capable of loving them back. It is with regret I cannot make her stay longer.

14
Mine

Believing myself out of options and too old to continue justifying a cavalier approach to life, I re-entered the workforce at twenty-seven. A clerk making $12 an hour at a payday loan center, it was here I forgot my basketball fantasies. It was time to act like a grown-up and remember I did not come from money or privileged circumstances.

The next step in remembering, I supposed, was to find my own place. Research led me to an income-based program that would subsidize a large portion of my rent. I could choose any participating apartment complex and chose one in Portage—a town bordering Gary—I wouldn't have otherwise been able to afford after spending my first few years out of college chasing childhood instead of adulting. The neighborhood had far less crime, better infrastructure, and cleaner streets. It was quiet. I applied without telling anyone.

"I'm moving out," I said to my mom the day I received word my application was approved.

"Oh . . . okay. Where?" she asked.

"To these apartments in Portage."

"Well, *congratulaaations*," she sang.

End of discussion.

I signed my lease, got my keys, and walked over to check out my new digs. The hallway leading to my third-floor unit smelled funny; it made me think of visiting Grandmama's all those years ago. Someone must've had chitterlings, neck bones, and ham hocks boiling on the stove. The carpeted stairs were dark, tattered and worn. But when I opened the door to my unit it was bright with sunshine beaming through the windows. The carpet smelled new, and the appliances were modern.

Mine. All mine.

I walked into the bedroom and slid open the mirrored closet doors. The smell of fresh paint escaped. I stepped across the hall and entered the bathroom, flicked the light on and stared at *my* shower, *my* toilet, *my* towel rack, thinking about how I'd decorate the space.

In the kitchen, I peered inside the eggshell-colored refrigerator as though something might be in there. I turned on every heating coil on the electric stove to ensure each worked. I walked through the living room and out the sliding patio door. From the cherrywood deck, I surveyed my new community, taking note of the trash area and the pool behind the leasing office before returning inside. I stretched my body across the dining room and made snow angels along the carpet until dozing off.

Upon awakening to darkness and cold, I hopped up from the floor and dragged my hand against the wall until it touched a light switch. One last look around reawakened my butterflies. I couldn't wait to be unbothered indefinitely, in my entire living space, not just in my bedroom.

Independence: was that the thing on the other side of my longing? Or was it isolation? I wanted to be alone, more alone than I'd always been. More aloneness than I'd found locking myself in my bedroom away from family. Because in aloneness nothing was expected of me and there was no one for me to expect anything of, and this meant we could not let each other down.

I didn't have a single piece of furniture outside of my bedroom set, or a clue as to how I might obtain such items, and didn't care. I'd sit on the floor, on my brand-new carpet, if it was the only option for me to move in right away.

Back at my mother's house, I slept in my room with posters of Immature and basketball players covering the wall, for the final night. The next morning Richard loaded up a truck with my few items—a bed, dresser, television, desk—and set it all up at my new place. I had a housewarming party for which my mother did what she does, crafted and decorated until plain spaces turned lovely. Timika's mom gifted me a couch. Eventually, I bought a cheap dining set and plastic TV stand from a discount store called Big Lots. It all came together.

I called Jason to tell him about my new place.

"Yo, who dis?" he answered.

"Who is this? It's Camey!"

"Oh," he snickered. "I deleted your number."

"Dang. Why?"

"Because you made it clear you weren't interested. I deleted the number so I couldn't reach out again, even if I wanted to. I ain't no simp!"

"Okay, okay. I can accept that." We both laughed.

Jason came to check out my apartment and even stayed over a few nights. We reconnected for a spell, but it ended the same because I was the same. Nothing had changed except an understanding that Jason would not be kept at arm's length, nor would he force his way forward. It was fun while it lasted, however. More fun without pressure and expectations.

Jason and I spent entire weekends together now, because the day I moved out was also the day I stopped going to church. I'd already reduced my attendance, but when you live in someone else's home, you sometimes do things to appease them out of respect. This is especially true when that someone is a parent.

As a kid, even a teenage one, I was required to attend church every Sunday. Once older, with my own car, job, and commitments, I went less and less. Some Sundays my mother wouldn't say anything. Some Sundays she would. She'd knock on my bedroom door until I responded, "Yeah?"

"You should come to church."

She'd knock again and repeat the suggestion a few minutes later as she left the house for Sunday School. Sometimes I'd peel myself from bed, slide into a back pew twenty minutes late, and leave immediately after the service.

At first, I simply wouldn't muster the energy. More than two decades of routine Sundays made me weary. Working during the week or when I was playing basketball left me cherishing off days. I wanted to sleep late and lie around watching my favorite shows.

Later, I lost any value I once found in going. Maybe I never saw value in it. Attending church was just something we did. With Grandma, with my mother, with a family full of minsters, pastors, bishops, choir members, praise dancers, and people for whom the Bible is law. It wasn't a choice.

Later still I questioned the point of church. I considered myself an integrous individual who did nothing with the aim of hurting anyone. A person who could not operate in bad faith with a clear conscience. A God who would send someone like me to hell simply because I didn't attend church was not a God I wished to serve.

For me it was enough to be a decent human, kind to other humans. I didn't care who you followed or what you believed.

Didn't need the dogma. How could everything *of the world* be labeled *of the devil* when listening to Whitney Houston had made me feel divine?

The Christmas I was gifted a Sony Discman led to me join-ing Columbia House Music Club and sending in those cards to get eight CDs for a penny. I hid the CDs under my bed. Not be-cause I wasn't fulfilling the paid obligation, but because I wasn't allowed to listen to secular music. Getting a Discman aided me in circumventing house rules.

The Bodyguard soundtrack was among my first selections. I remained in awe of Whitney Houston's fierce beauty and big voice after watching the accompanying movie with my mom and Terry. (The no secular music rule had loopholes.) I'd put my headphones on and fall asleep to her voice. I'd dream about her doing things with me a loving parent might do, cuddling and gig-gling, doting on me simply for being me. The gospel according to Nippy is where I found adolescent solace. I did not see how it could be wrong.

Religion saved my mother from herself, from her sadness and the demons fighting for control of her mind. She held on to a scripture Grandma drilled into her after San Diego, Romans 8:1. *There is therefore now no condemnation to those who are in Christ Jesus, who do not walk according to the flesh, but according to the Spirit.*

Religion offered my mother redemption without which she did not believe she could have forgiven herself and carried on with this life. She asked her savior to bear the cross she could not carry. Trusting a power greater than herself, immersing her-self in church, leaving her burdens at its altar, and adhering to its governing principles had been transformative for her. It's been transformative for many. I only decided it wasn't for me. I didn't believe like she did. Couldn't cling to things unseen like she could. Besides, Champ wore a cross around his neck and what did it mean? They are two sides of the same coin. *Good Christian* carried no greater weight with me than *good person*. And I'd seen enough to know the concepts were not synonymous.

I stayed in my first apartment for one year because during that year I was hired to work in the accounting department at United States Steel. When I needed to re-certify for the income-based program, they discovered my salary far exceeded the limit. My pay had increased from $12 an hour to $57,000 a year.

"Ummm, no, I'm sorry," the lady in the leasing office said while reviewing my paycheck stubs. "You no longer qualify for the program your unit is reserved for. You could move into a market-rent apartment, but we don't have any available." She poked her bottom lip out and gave me the sad face. "You're such a great tenant. We'd love to keep you. We just don't have the inventory."

"It's okay," I told the lady. "I figured as much."

If I'd had my way I would've stayed and enjoyed having more disposable income. Instead, I embarked on my first apartment search without really having to worry about cost. In 2007, I could afford to live anywhere in Northwest Indiana on my salary. Lake Pointe was the winner, a newer development down the street from where I already lived. It was lavish, with ducks swimming in a pond out front. Units had private entrances, which meant no smelly hallways or awkward encounters with other tenants. My bedroom was huge, with a walk-in closet and its own patio. There was a patio outside the living room, too.

It was surreal, making more money than I'd ever seen, more than anyone in my immediate family. But it didn't go as far once I began buying my way to worthiness, again. A few years after leasing my swanky apartment, I purchased a used Lexus GS 350. The price tag required an eighty-four-month loan to put my payments in the range of affordable. Negligible details. I slid into my black leather seats, retracted the sunroof, and floated away from the dealership.

My car was stunning.

Its shiny black exterior matched the interior. It had a woodgrain steering wheel, rear spoiler, and a huge touchscreen for the radio which included a five-disc CD changer. Everything was electric, not just the tinted windows. The seats, the sunshade, the trunk, every feature operated at the silent push of a button.

The looks I got hopping into and out of this car, while using the drive-thru window at fast food restaurants or passing people on the road, I hadn't gotten before. How others perceived and approached me changed quite literally overnight. People spoke to me with an air of respect and old men at the dealership or at car washes called me "ma'am" instead of "young lady." *Yes ma'am. No ma'am. Anything else I can do for you, ma'am?* They smiled at my Lexus and said things like, "Sweet ride!"

Behind the wheel of my luxury vehicle was a part of me afraid of again being that kid at the pencil sharpener, informed of her unfortunate place in the world and pitied for her audacious ignorance. The wind danced in her hair when she retracted her sunroof, and I understood. Holding something of tangible value can make those who've felt worthless, feel royal.

Even reaping all these fruits of my labor, I hated my job. I thought I'd be in the WNBA by now! Didn't think my undergraduate major would matter when I chose criminal justice.

Because U.S. Steel covered college tuition for employees, I went to grad school and got a master's degree in sports organization. My latest goal was to become an athlete agent. Then I learned most agents at that time were also attorneys, and I wanted no part of law school. Nonetheless, my interests were sports, storytelling, and marketing. Accounting is the opposite of creative. I was bored to numbness.

While appreciating my middle-class salary, I loathed the tasks I needed to complete in earning it. "I'm dying at my job," I told Timika. "What!" she replied. She didn't understand and I couldn't explain. Getting into a steel mill was the goal for those living in the region. I'm sure whining about purpose and fulfillment from the comfort of my Lexus sounded to others like me playing the tiniest violin.

I also despised my environment, how it reminded me mostly of things I wished to forget. Though I technically didn't live in Gary anymore, I lived close enough to feel like I did, and I worked in the city. Maybe even more than at my job, it felt like I was dying in this town.

Gary has represented your typical urban jungle for a while, but especially now. Overcome with poverty, the city is riddled with burned down and forsaken buildings, uninhabited housing communities, and roads destroyed by potholes. It's estimated about one-third of all homes are abandoned or unoccupied. Every single school I attended in my hometown has closed its doors. Yet, there's a liquor store within a few blocks of wherever you might be. Not as many as there once were, however. Not even businesses that profit from despair could survive Gary's collapse, given there were fewer residents left to exploit.

I don't mean to trash my native land. Or speak as though it no longer holds anything good. We still have a beautiful beach. Can still boast that two of the greatest entertainers to ever exist are from our city. We still have passionate educators, service workers, and community members committed to the idea that Gary can be great again. There is goodness left, it just became near impossible to see.

Gary's population was 69,093 as of the 2020 census, a sixty-one percent drop from its peak of 178,320 in 1960. The once-prosperous steel town experienced this rapid population decline as overseas competition increased and undercut U.S. production costs, leading to thousands of workers being let go. Without the life-changing income, there wasn't much reason to stay— and little other way to financially sustain the decision if you tried.

I look at photos of a bustling 1960s Gary with awe for a place I wished I'd known. Broadway, the main street downtown, was lined with businesses, shops, and a movie theatre. It was lined with people, shuffling about with briefcases or families in tow. Today, the internet refers to Gary as a ghost town.

We have a long history of taking what's given to us and flipping it to our perceived advantage. Thus, many peers were proud of the "Murder Capital" title. It was a badge of honor for those who hung their self-worth on being feared and viewed respect as something taken by force. My McDonald's boyfriend-turned-rapper bragged about the label in his lyrics.

Combine the engulfing deterioration with believing myself stuck inside one of the only well-paying jobs available, and my urge to get out of Gary grew unignorable. I needed more opportunities, more people, different people, more life. I needed to forget everyone here, especially those who'd forgotten me.

My survival seemed tied to moving not only minutes but thousands of miles from the site of my earliest encounters with bottomless anguish. I needed to leave the place where I learned to ask if I was good enough. Upping the ante on my solitude seemed a solid solution.

I held the ambiguous idea of relocating in the back of my mind for a while. Then the death of my grandmother brought it to the front. *One of these days* became *this day.*

Grandma had always talked about her "ship coming in." She was certain it would happen. To support her belief, she enrolled in college when well into her sixth decade of life, studied art history, and became a collector. She was the oldest student in her classes, perhaps in the school. She told Danny and me that meant she had to work twice as hard as everyone else when she shuffled to the dining room at night carrying armfuls of books.

Years later, both having acquired at least one higher education degree, neither of us was living our respective dreams. But Grandma kept learning, kept believing, and kept collecting paintings for more than ten years, until health issues consumed her seventies and she could no longer drive or do much writing and researching.

There was no long, drawn out battle with illness or a terminal diagnosis. Her death was sudden, in her sleep. She died before the ship she'd worked to materialize could manifest.

The day passed in flashes. A cracking voicemail from my mother. A crawl from bed to my living room floor. A mindless drive to the hospital. Suddenly, I was just there, looking at her little lifeless body, open-mouthed like she was about to speak. I went home and cried more than I ever remembered crying as an adult.

I thought about her legacy. What she instilled in me. How grateful I was to get my no nonsense, no excuses attitude from her.

I did not get her ability to harness hope which, coming from where I'm from, is its own miracle. Its own opulence. It is triumph in the face of persistent disaster. Grandma achieved this, found a way to live in her imagination. I could not. My hope had limits. Despite all I'd accomplished in and around Gary, I couldn't see past it. Couldn't see myself thriving in the belly of previous trauma.

The abrupt disappearance of the woman who raised me cut the thread by which I was hanging on to an area that aroused only bitter thoughts of loss, poverty, and neglect. I wanted to know a world where people flourished and became who they set out to become. It's difficult to start a new chapter in the confines of a city where every page of the book reads the same. I wanted a new book.

"You gone leave that good job?" was the most common response I received when informing family and friends I planned to move across the country. I understood their astonishment. When you live with scarcity as your dominant mindset, you're afraid to let go of what you have for fear nothing else will come along.

Still, less than a year after Grandma's funeral, I packed up my posh Portage apartment, hired movers, and had all my things transported more than 1700 miles to Las Vegas, Nevada. Timika and her parents were settled there. She helped me find a nice spot to stay, ready upon my arrival.

Relocating so far from the place you've known as home, unaccompanied, might be a huge step for most. I wasn't planted with such deep roots. Sure, I loved people as much as I could given my limited exposure to, and understanding of, the concept. But I'd felt all by myself in the presence of most of those people. Living fifteen minutes away from Gary in Portage, I rarely saw most of them. We may as well have been time zones apart. So, why not?

There were no discussions. No weighing of pros and cons or tying up loose ends. I'd visited Vegas and only saw pros— warm weather, bigger city, beautiful landscape, various career paths, and a chance to reinvent myself.

"Why so far away?" my mother asked.

"I like it," was all the reason I offered in return.

"Mecca will miss you," she said.

Mecca was the only person in my family I spent time with on a regular basis. When I left for Vegas, she was seven years old, just around the age I was when my sense of abandonment began to balloon. I'd committed to showing up for her, doing all I could to help ensure she didn't share my childhood experiences. We went to movies, restaurants, carnivals, everywhere. I bought her name-brand clothes and shoes for school. I seized any opportunity to tell her, "I love you." Everything I'd wished someone had done for me at that age, I did for her. I'd miss Mecca too and vowed to bring her to Vegas every single summer, to show her there's a great big world outside Gary.

15
Safe Room

An official Nevadan, I adapted to my new sunshine-filled lifestyle. I was doing things I'd never done, like jogging around a park every morning. It was gorgeous, with green grass, paved trails, and basketball courts that had nets and rims still attached! All the equipment was operable and aesthetically pleasing. I'd pass women walking their dogs or pushing strollers and see men tossing Frisbees to their kids. Everyone seemed at peace, including me.

Yoga was another hobby I picked up. Sessions sometimes took place outside, at the same park, under the most magnificent sunsets I'd witnessed. The orange ball of fire looked closer than ever as we shifted from tree pose to downward dog, like it might be possible to get close enough to touch as it retreated behind a ridge of red mountains.

In Vegas I felt reborn. I joined Meetup groups and talked to strangers, went hiking, and spent the entire summer at pool parties. I found work in the marketing department at a casino and got to be creative for a living. I discovered everything I'd arrived in search of.

Having extended time with Mecca was icing on the rejuvenated cake. She's a pretty cool kid to hang out with. I've held fast to my promise of bringing her to visit every summer. As much as she probably believes I've given her, she's given me much more. When she's here I am the best, most purposeful version of myself. For those three or four weeks we go on a series of adventures. I'd taken Mecca to her first WNBA game. We go hiking and to live shows, and we always end her visits with dinner at a hibachi grill.

"You're the best auntie ever," she told me. I locked those words away in the safest corner of my spirit. I'd done one relationship right.

My apartment lost some luster when I took Mecca to the airport and returned home to clean the evidence of her presence. I deflated the air mattress on my living room floor and put it away. I threw out all the kid-friendly food. There were no sounds of anime or SpongeBob SquarePants blaring from the television. That night, the next morning and those following, I would go back to making one-person meals.

Whether or not Mecca was in Vegas, Gary seemed a world away. Aside from Kasey, contact with anyone still there was limited. I talked to my mother and brother intermittently, often about Mecca. I hadn't thought about my father in years, until my stepsister sent me a Facebook message. This was unusual. We rarely talked outside of family gatherings.

"I heard Adrienne passed this morning. I am so sorry." She apologized to me. Why? Because Adrienne and I share a father? I'd expect to be the one offering, not receiving condolences. I expressed general concern and sympathy, as I would've had the news been about anyone. Though it felt like I should ask what happened.

"I'm not sure of the exact timeline," she responded. "I just know she passed in the middle of the night. If I get more info, I will pass it along." I told her I'd appreciate it. Then a few days later my stepsister sent information for the services taking place in Indiana.

"Are you going to make it?" she asked.

"I don't think so."

I suppose it was my fault she thought I might fly across the country and attend the funeral. I had led her on with my politeness. I forgot most people don't express sympathy without sentiment, or ask clarifying questions without intent. Most people don't say things only because they think they should say them. Yet, I found it bizarre, the idea that I would travel almost two thousand miles to pay respects or say goodbye to someone I barely knew when she was alive. Is it bizarre? Or am I callous? I couldn't decide.

By August 2014, Adrienne and I hadn't seen or spoken with one another in almost a decade. I wondered if my stepsister was aware Adrienne and I had never acknowledged our relation during our few months at college together. I wondered if it mattered. Is this something people do? Go to funerals and feign connection where it does not exist because others think it should?

I thought about my former teammate's words after the death of her grandmother. How hesitant Krystal had been to share her innermost thoughts for fear of being perceived as cold. It's how my stepsister must've viewed me in the apathy-filled moment when I revealed I would not be present at the services.

Whether or not Champ knew crossed my mind. I speculated on whether they'd been in touch. History suggests they hadn't. But I hoped Adrienne died knowing love from someone.

I contemplated my own demise. If I met my end, alone in my apartment, on the other side of the country from all the people I pushed away, would anyone notice? The bigger question: Did I care?

I've lied.

Wait. Lie is a strong, definitive word. I haven't been untruthful. What I've done is lack transparency.

Moving to Vegas hasn't been a skip down the yellow brick road. Things started as ideally as I've implied with the yoga and the exercise and the basking in abundant sunshine, the sun that washes over me when I step outside and makes me feel pristine enough to warrant all the good things. But I don't go outside much anymore.

I present my relocation journey as smooth sailing because I cannot bear to acknowledge or admit that issues from Gary have followed me here. As the novelty of my new home fades, I'm forced to face familiar foes. The idea of taking such radical action only to end up laboring beneath similar weight makes it seem heavier. I'm not carrying it well.

I want to believe it's all better now. I fixed it. I want you to believe it too. The whole truth is, moving across the country has been a mixed bag and a slow grind. It hit a momentary reset button in my life, but hasn't afforded a lasting solution.

I'd arrived in Vegas at the end of 2011, with the economy climbing its way out of ruin. But I didn't know anything about the economy, or the housing market, or the job market. I was barely thirty years old, hailing from a place and people with limited financial literacy. I hadn't considered any of those things because I didn't *know* to consider them. Plus, I'd been making a solid middle-class income in Gary, living in a fancy apartment, and driving a Lexus. Things were looking good to me!

It would take almost three years to land that casino marketing job. In the meantime, I'd burn through my savings and run up credit cards—piling new burdens on top of the old ones and feeding fresh anxieties. I'd contribute to magazines and websites for minimal compensation as a freelance writer. A temp agency would send me on assignments here and there until I was eventually hired part-time as the executive assistant to a local businessman. About six months later I'd get laid off. Then, finally, after almost a year of collecting unemployment, the casino would come calling.

This can't be life. It certainly isn't the one I signed up for and gave up all I had to live. Because if it is, and all the world has to offer me is here, I humbly decline.

It feels like I'm dying, again. Yes, things are difficult. But I've done difficult, conquered it on many occasions. Difficult might exhaust me, though sometimes it also invigorates me. What it does not do is break me.

I think the culprit is my shattered subconscious belief that I wouldn't have to fight all these private battles anymore. It's the unfulfilled hope that someone might save me even if I don't need saving; or at least stand by my side as I fight. I wouldn't bore them with my troubles, but knowing my troubles aren't a bore would be nice.

I think it's this persistent aloneness. This solitude. It's killing me. I'm trapped inside my safe room.

Thing is, you don't know you're trapped until you try to get out and realize you can't. Moving to Vegas was my attempt at escape. Yet here I am in the same place I've always been, the emotional isolation that once served as my protection.

I'm staring out into the twilight behind my sliding glass patio doors. How fatefully cruel to find myself back here, gazing out at a world carrying on without me, glaring at nothing, waiting for something to appear.

This is the part where I admit I'm broken.

The little girl inside me didn't make the trip. She remains in Gary. She continues resisting forgiveness and sidestepping compassion. She's holding on to the worst of all she endured there, determined to make it known to everyone she meets. I regurgitate her story to anyone who will listen and call it healing. San Diego, Kareem, neglect, I tell them everything.

There are no violent crying spells, yet I am again the kid pondering why she's sunk so low. Then I'm the kid no longer searching for the reason, simply wanting it to stop. Who should I ask to rid me of this darkness? I've tried God, already. I've prayed. Not for an easy life but for wounds that heal, cracks that fix. I've tried all I can think to try.

I've learned there are things I can actively do to pick myself up. I don't have to just wish for relief. Practicing yoga, outdoor exercise, and following the work of self-help gurus like Paulo Coelho and Thich Nhat Hanh worked for a little while. It turns out the teachings of Eastern Philosophy resonate with me. But this strain of gloom has grown resistant. Something is holding on, has always held on, and has reemerged so I know it has not set me free. It's been weeks since my last sun salutation. I haven't cared to open a book. Nor have I found the energy for once peaceful jogs around the park. I don't want to do anything, ever.

I surrender. You win, life. Flawless victory. I haven't a single trophy to show for my trials.

My childhood offered many contributions to a life of melancholy. To rest the entire responsibility with my father would be disingenuous, though to absolve him would be just as foolish. I wanted him at some point. I waited for him. His never coming tainted my view of the world, of people, of myself.

My father's absence didn't matter much to me in adulthood.

But it mattered to her, that little girl. No one ever stopped her bleeding.

I needed help. Actual help. It was the last thought I remembered thinking before a blinding Vegas sunlight slipped through the blinds and danced on my face, forcing me to rise.

I picked up my phone and scrolled through social media. Without much of an objective, I tweeted a desire to learn meditation and continued scrolling. An almost immediate reply notification came through.

A writer friend responded with information on Transcendental Meditation, including his personal experience. He called the practice "life changing" and encouraged me to check it out.

I was at the Las Vegas TM Center a couple of days later.

"There's a sadness in your eyes," the TM instructor commented within minutes of meeting me.

I could smile. I could sit in silence. I could behave as everyone around me, but my eyes could never lie.

The teacher sat in a chair facing mine. She wore glasses, an ankle-length dress, and a shoulder-length haircut with bangs and streaks of gray. Her hands folded neatly in her lap. She spoke in a slow, soft voice.

"Why are you here, Acamea? Why are you so sad?"

The teacher lifted a hand from her lap and extended it toward me. For a minute she didn't say anything else. She just held my hand and looked into my eyes. The room was dimly lit with the smoke and aroma of a burning candle floating through the air. I might have squirmed if it weren't so serene.

I broke eye contact and looked down at the floor. "I don't know," I said. It's the same answer I'd given to the same question my entire life.

The instructor gently stroked the top of my hand with her

thumb. "I've studied your responses to our questionnaire. Based on your educational background, struggles you shared, and what I've picked up on sitting here with you, I'm going to give you a mantra. I want you to repeat it over and over in your head when I tell you to. Okay?"

I nodded.

She gave me the mantra and asked me to say it aloud. "Now close your eyes. Repeat it in your head until I tell you to stop."

The instructor and the room faded. It was escape, followed by relief. For those fifteen minutes, I was free.

During our session, tears flowed from my eyes, and I didn't resist. I couldn't resist. Something inside me had reached its tipping point.

I didn't notice what was happening or remember what I was doing until my time expired, and the lady whispered, "Open your eyes." With a faint smile and raised eyebrows she asked, "How do you feel?"

I felt a surprising lightness. Like I could breathe easy. Like my heart wasn't a boulder inside my body. Like I might just be alright. But I responded, "Fine."

The instructor's smile widened. She knew. "Fine" was an exceptional understatement.

The waterworks happened often during the first month of my practice. I didn't know where it came from, but I always felt better afterward. This wasn't like the uncontrollable, draining sobbing. This was release.

I was functioning again. I'd say I was joyful again, but it felt like the first time. Being overwhelmed with gratitude at the presence of flowers and overtaken by the brilliance of a sunrise, made me unsure if I'd ever known happiness at all.

I felt alive and cared that I did. Lows weren't as low. Highs not as high. A middle ground, balance, is what I found.

16
Trading Ghost Stories

A guy asked me on our first date, "Would you rather have an absent father or a shit-but-present father?" Before answering, I pondered whether it's possible one can be an absent but not a shit father? Can you neglect a life you helped bring into the world and it not warrant classification as a crappy parent? I get what he was asking, however. Often the parent who is present enough to traumatize you on a consistent basis leaves more destruction in their wake than the one who vacates their post altogether.

Fatherhood always comes up somehow, someway during introductory conversations. It's a natural progression. When getting to know someone, you ask where they're from and inquire about their family. So, when people ask about my mom and dad, my response involves revealing I haven't seen the latter since I was a small child. The answer opens a whole new box of questions. They want to know how such a thing happened and what it triggers inside me.

178 ~ *Daddy's Little Stranger*

On many occasions, my revelation has led the other person to offer similar disclosures. All these men and women with strained, problematic, or non-existent relationships with their fathers. So many of us ashamed to share our stories because it still makes some part of us feel inadequate.

As much as I've worked to ditch the victimhood that can attach itself to fatherlessness, it seems intent on coming along for the ride. It might not be driving the car but sits in the passenger seat, waiting for me to ask what it thinks. It stares at me from across tables and the other side of rooms. It eavesdrops on the frequent conversations I find myself having on the topic—smiling, eager for its turn in the spotlight.

Thus, I may overcompensate. I might overemphasize my fineness with my fatherlessness and the disconnection from half my heritage. Because I sense the victimhood there, lurking. Ready and waiting for me to feel bad or blue, or sorry for myself.

The person I'm speaking to usually looks at me as though you would a lost puppy, no matter how emotionlessly I deliver the story. They look at me like I have DADDY ISSUES stamped across my forehead. Like they want to hug me. I loathe this expression and make avoiding it my ultimate priority.

Sometimes though, my approach is deadpan because I'm aware some details might seem sad. I don't know particulars about myself others deem important. Things people expect me to know or at least care to know. It's like I have a missing piece but am attempting to pass the puzzle off as complete.

I tried a new spot for lunch. After grabbing my order, I sat at a booth near the entryway. With one hand I ate my crab cake and my carrot ginger soup. With the other, I read a book.

A guy entered the restaurant. I saw him lingering nearby but didn't look up. "Excuse me," a voice said. "Can I ask you a question?"

I lifted my head to see a tall, bearded bald guy wearing medical scrubs. "How's the book?" he asked. We chatted about *The*

Mastery Of Love by Don Miguel Ruiz for a bit, though it was clear he only used the book as a conversation starter.

The guy offered his name before requesting mine. "Where are you from?" he asked. I revealed myself a Las Vegas local, a necessary distinction when you live in a tourist town. "I'm originally from Indiana," I added.

He took a step toward me and abruptly clarified. "No, I mean what's your ethnicity?"

It's a question I often get. People survey my light skin, hazel-brown eyes, fuzzy hair, and assume I'm the product of interracial parents. They ask what I'm "mixed with."

I responded to him the way I respond to them all. "I'm one hundred percent Black . . . that I know of." Because I really don't know, it seems disingenuous to put it out there as a certainty.

My biological father has a Hispanic first name. When a relationship evolves and I share this tidbit, the other person has an aha moment. They try to convince me both my father and I are of Latin descent.

The guy at the restaurant also had a Hispanic name. He gave me a surprised, skeptical look when I didn't declare mixed heritage. I just raised my eyebrows. Next, he asked for my phone number to arrange for us to "meet up and talk about the book."

I very well could be of entirely African descent. We produce various skin tones, hair textures, and eye colors. Deviations from commonalities don't explicitly signal genetics of a different race. It's just that only knowing the full ethnicity of one of my parents, I've never had even the most basic details to support either conclusion, and have never cared to learn more.

I think about the day I arrived for an appointment with my hairstylist, Lauren. She said hello and asked how I was doing. I returned the pleasantry and planted myself atop her styling seat. Lauren responded, "Fine," but her tone said otherwise.

My stylist was always upbeat when I came in, striking up lively conversation as soon as I entered her private room in the salon. Today however, her voice was low, and her responses were short. Her movements unfolded almost in slow motion, as though it took considerable energy to tie a protective cape around my neck and spin the chair toward the sink.

I twisted to look back at Lauren. She wasn't visibly flustered, but her face was blank, staring down into a distance. She didn't even noticed I'd turned to look at her.

After a few moments, I pierced the silence with, "Are you okay?" It jerked her back into the room with me. Lauren jumped, pushed her glasses up her nose, and fixed her eyes onto mine as though she only then remembered I was there.

"I used Ancestry DNA to find my father," she answered. I perked up and wanted to smile but could sense I shouldn't. Lauren continued with a measured recount of the story.

"Yeah, girl. He's a white man. First, I found an aunt, then his mother. My grandmother. I called and talked to them on the phone. They were nice. The aunt wants to come out here for a visit."

Her voice trailed off.

"They told me he died a few years ago."

Lauren's gaze fell again. I slumped down in my seat while she sluggishly shampooed my hair. We both stayed quiet for a few minutes. Me, stretched backward, fixated on the ceiling. Her, towering above, lost in the wash bowl.

It was too late. Lauren's excitement was almost immediately suffocated by sorrow. She met and mourned her father in the same moment—though she wasn't allowed the tangible experience of either event.

"At least I found out he was white," Lauren said.

We talked about how she always gets the same questions about her ethnicity as I do. Until now, she'd responded the way

I did. Her identity, everything she knew about herself, changed. Lauren held burning questions that would remain unanswered. She had a void she was now certain would remain unfilled.

"I'm glad I met his family," Lauren said. "I've been meeting more people every day. They all want to talk to me! At least I have some closure, I guess. Knowing he's dead."

"It doesn't make you feel better, that you found him?" I asked.

"No," Lauren said. "Because of how it ended. I wanted to *know* him. I just keep thinking, what if I had done this sooner?"

I told her about my own journey as a fatherless daughter. Having someone who could relate, who saw her, I think lifted Lauren's spirits. We spoke with disdain about how a parent could forsake their child, and with compassion for how it affected us. It's like we were trading ghost stories. Then Lauren asked, "You've never tried to find your dad?"

I suppressed a scoff of laughter and answered, "No." It wasn't the question I found laughable, but the notion that I might look for him. My stylist was confused.

I explained how I'd lived without my father an overwhelming majority of my years. I had no alternate state of being to compare the condition against. It'd been a long time since I'd sensed a void. Plus, I felt I'd turned out well without his influence.

"Yeah, you have an icebox where your heart used to be," was Lauren's response. It made us both chuckle.

"Maybe."

My rationale was that you can't miss what you never had. But my stylist missed what she never had and was disappointed to discover she'd never have it. How could comparable experiences affect us so differently?

I went home thinking about our conversation. I thought about the distress, how it choked away Lauren's voice. Her aching, mourning, and unrequited longing for her estranged father stayed with me. I contemplated why I didn't have that.

Would I rather have an absent father or a shit-but-present father? After much deliberation, I choose absent. But I don't know. Even the question, to me, the intrigue, signals someone who's had neither.

17

#GirlDad

I was having dinner with Iris in a Florida hotel when the story broke. She leaned over and said it to me in a loud whisper, as though it shouldn't be said aloud but the shock couldn't be fully contained. "Girl! Kobe Bryant died!"

"What? How?"

"I don't know," she said. "Gabe just texted me."

Her husband's newsflash prompted me to get on social media and Iris, who doesn't do social, to visit a news website. There it was: a helicopter crash had killed Bryant, his thirteen-year-old daughter Gianna, and seven more beloved humans.

I stammered out, "Oh no. His wife. His kids. And one of them died. Her mother. This is devastating."

"Right!" Iris said. "I can't believe it. So sad. I always try to think of the reason behind these situations, you know? Why God allows it to happen."

Iris is not religious but believes in God, leans on God for clarity, comfort, and direction. She was convinced there must be something we weren't aware of concerning why. A reason Kobe had to go. "You never know," she said.

"Okay, but what about his daughter?" I asked. "What could be the reason for her dying so young?"

"Maybe God knew she wouldn't have been able to make it without her father," Iris replied. "They were so close. Maybe he knew it would've been too much for her, but his other girls and his wife could handle it." She shrugged.

I shrugged and turned the conversation back to lamenting the devastation rather than contemplating pseudo justifications. I got why she took the approach. I've long comprehended the need to have something to hold on to, and on many occasions wished I had something that applied purpose to otherwise senseless pain.

"Your father is Hispanic," Iris asserted as she drove me to the airport.

Our conversation about Kobe and his daughters had led to discussing my biological father. More specifically, my not knowing much about him and taking no action to learn more.

"I think you should," Iris said. "Because you never know. You feel this way now but you could change your mind. You might regret not finding him when you had the chance."

What about Champ finding me? is what I think when people say stuff like this. Then I remember he once tried.

"The only reason I've ever even thought about it is to learn my full ethnicity," I said to Iris.

I told her Champ's full name. She glanced over at me, face scrunched in a *you can't be serious* manner. "I can tell."

"I don't think I look Hispanic," I said.

"Yes, you do. You look like my in-laws. Your features. And your hair isn't kinky-curly. I can tell. You look like Gabe's family."

I stopped debating both topics, my ethnicity and whether I should find Champ. Iris is an attorney. She argues for a living and doesn't let things go until her burden of proof is satisfied. As we approached the terminal, she was still going.

"I'm just saying. You should really think about it, Camey."

We got out of the car to hug goodbye.

"Maybe."

Less than a year before the accident, Mecca and I saw Kobe and Gigi (as Gianna was called) at a Las Vegas Aces WNBA basketball game. The arena put them up on the jumbotron. Kobe beamed, Gigi laughed and somewhat shied away from the camera. Without realizing it right away, I stood grinning at the screen like an amazed idiot, thinking how sweet it was he'd brought his daughter to a game. Witnessing nothing but this, I already loved the way he loved her. He was guiding her, a budding basketball star, down the path he'd masterfully traveled.

Many would say Kobe was only doing what a father should do. Well, I'd say many don't know what it's like to grow up fatherless. To us, it's something. Small gestures in the eyes of others represent monumental gaps in the timeline of our lives.

When #GirlDad dominated social media following an anecdote from ESPN analyst Elle Duncan, I was obsessed with the trend. If you haven't heard, the gist of the story is this: Duncan asked the sports icon for advice as she was pregnant with a baby girl. Kobe, who at that time had three daughters and no sons, mentioned his wife Vanessa wanted to try for a boy but was afraid it wouldn't happen. Duncan asked how he would take it if they did try and ended up with yet another daughter. Kobe's response was, "I would have five more girls if I could. I'm a girl dad."

I came undone. Duncan's voice cracking, the sweetness of Kobe's proclamation, the tenderness of the recollection and the circumstance prompting it ignited a visceral dismantling. While he's an undisputed NBA legend, Kobe the father will always be my favorite.

As Duncan's emotional tribute went viral, fathers flooded Twitter with pictures of their daughters alongside #GirlDad. I spent hours scrolling through them all. Dads tweeted photos of themselves with their baby girls, older girls, and full-grown women who would always be their little girls. The pictures stirred within me a euphoria infiltrated by grief.

I must've retweeted at least ten of the photos. Some were of celebrity girl dads like Alex Rodriguez, Russell Wilson, and LeVar Burton. Others displayed unfamiliar dads and girls who looked to adore one another.

The word most used in the more than 175,000 #GirlDad tweets those first few days was *love*.

Observing such an overwhelming, endless stream of proud fathers laying public claim to their daughters—to the apparent incredible fortune of being a girl dad—felt like studying a phenomenon up close. It's true, you can appreciate the magnificence of sunshine that has never warmed your skin. We can identify splendor in moments reminding us of those we've lost.

I was obsessed with the visual representation of father-daughter connections as much for my finding it peculiar as for my finding it sublime. The dynamic remains strange to me. I looked at the photos and tried to imagine what their relationships might have been like.

Do they hug and kiss? These two are looking at each other instead of at the camera so, probably. Look how tightly the dad's arms are wrapped around his daughter. Wow, he has five daughters. They're all smiling. Did they grow up feeling protected? Would this daughter have come to the phone if her dad left at some point and later returned to make amends?

They were dad girls. All of them. I could tell by looking at their photos, analyzing their relaxed body language, examining how they existed in the captured moment. They were fundamentally different from me.

To be loved simply because you're you. Because you're a girl. I imagine it must irrevocably validate your existence.

Once done scrolling through #GirlDad on Twitter, I closed my eyes. Later, with replenished energy, I went to Facebook and typed my father's name into the search bar. It was the only day in my adult life I'd felt compelled to locate him. I had no intention of reaching out but wanted to see his whereabouts and what he'd been up to. Seconds later, there he was, among less than a handful of people who share his half-Spanish/half-English name.

His face remained familiar. I'm the spitting image of my mother but recognized the one feature I'd inherited from my father, those chipmunk cheeks. He sat sideways in his photo and looked unaware it was about to be taken, like when someone calls your name and you turn your head to look their way, unprepared and off-guard.

I clicked on the photo and went to his profile. He lived in Nashville, Tennessee. Maybe he was there when I lived in Memphis. Maybe he passed through, and we crossed paths. What would he have thought of me? Daddy's little stranger.

Either Champ didn't post much or there wasn't much I could access without being his Facebook friend. There was almost no info aside from location, age, and the listless photograph. I studied the sparsely populated page for a few minutes before smashing my laptop shut.

Seeing him satisfied whatever I'd hoped to achieve. I was starting to notice what my stylist felt surfacing inside me. Only it was for the bond, not the person with whom I didn't have it.

Later that same year, Danny's father sent me a friend request. I hadn't called him Daddy in decades. It was the first time I'd heard from him since receiving a stream of tweets in early

2015 that began with, "Hey my daughter, how are you doing?"

He still saw me that way?

"Hey. I'm pretty good. How are you?"

"I am good," he tweeted.

From there he sent a couple of replies to my serious tweets, responded *LOL* to my silly ones, and wished me happy birthday. A month later, I heard from him again.

"Wow I still didn't get a happy birthday from you!"

"Sorry! I didn't know. Happy Birthday!!! Hope you enjoyed." *smiley face*

No response.

Towards the end of the year, he asked, "Hey, you talked with your brother lately?"

"Hey," I said. "Yes, I talked to Danny a couple of days ago actually. What's up?"

No response.

What was the point of this contact?

Then in 2020, the year of #GirlDad, I got the Facebook friend request. Perhaps the trend reminded him of me. A few messages followed, from December to June.

"Merry Christmas."

"Happy New Year."

"Happy birthday."

I was warming up to the idea of meeting him if he wanted to meet. Or talking with him if he wanted to talk. Maybe I could find my way back to viewing him as Daddy. What once seemed implausible appeared a mere challenge. But his sporadic contact followed by disappearing wouldn't allow me to get as comfortable as I would need to be for that to happen. I know, I pushed him away when I was younger. Maybe this relationship was on me to repair. Our communication ended with me saying, "Thank you" for the birthday wishes.

Next, I found myself sitting in front of my computer scrolling through pictures on Terry's social media pages, thinking *this could've been us*. It could've been me standing in a photo with my brother who attends a rival university, and our grandmother, sandwiched between us, wearing a *house divided* shirt. It could've been me posted on his wall with a proud pops message about my good grades and bright future. Terry's two children seemed wonderful. I like to think we could've been wonderful, too.

Women were fawning over my mother's longtime ex-boyfriend in the comment section of his selfies. It was all, "Hey tall, dark, and handsome," and "Looking good, Mr. Man." I could've been the daughter saying "Eww," embarrassed and bewildered people saw him as someone other than a dad. I almost was.

I sat imagining myself in the shoes of another man's adult children, despite knowing not having a father at this point is at least partially my doing. The nobody-wants-me claim can never be mine. Yet, this has never solely been about being wanted. Remember, Kareem showed me the dark side of desire. This is about being held in someone's heart—in a space saved especially for you. I wanted to feel worth fighting for.

Chicken or the egg? I debated with myself. Did I stop caring about family ties because I didn't have them? Or did I not have them because I didn't care? Did I truly miss having a father?

If we didn't see jovial families on TV and in movies, sitting around having dinner or tender talks, I question how differently we might absorb the idea of not having a similar home life. Because if no one ever told us we should have two parents around, divergent scenarios might not be as jarring. Much of the damage starts in our minds and rushes down to our hearts. Or maybe it's the other way. Maybe it starts in our hearts and festers in our minds.

I asked Kasey what she gained from her father that she wouldn't have without him. "My daddy taught me to stay calm in pressure-filled situations," she said. "I've never seen him give up or feel sorry for himself. It trained me to push through. To make things happen. But really, to understand what he gave me . . . to understand who my father is, you have to understand who my mother is."

Kasey's father is the antithesis of her mother. He is strong where she struggles and moves forward where she hesitates. That's part of it too. You often get a more proportionate upbringing with two parents, instead of everything being skewed to a particular approach. One parent is more affectionate, lenient, or communicative than the other. They each fill the gaps left by their counterparts, leaving you with fewer holes in your experience.

Family structures continue to evolve, though. A two-parent upbringing is no longer presumed an exclusive mother-father dynamic. Some kids have two dads, or two moms, a gender fluid or trans parent—and feel absolute love. They feel whole, safe, and seen. So, the problem isn't simply not having a biologically male father. It can't be.

I think the issue is mostly believing we've been discarded and taking it to mean we're bad or broken or difficult. It's needing to understand why. Because if the only people seemingly obligated to care for us, do not, what does it say about us?

I've unraveled the shift from believing you're fine one moment to searching for a place you aren't sure exists in the next. I get it. I grasp how fatherless daughters cope, and break, and heal, and reconcile in vastly different ways. I understand why my stylist might reach for relationship—while the best I can reach for right now is social media sightings. The furthest I can go is imagining what it might be like if we had a champion who would take to Twitter and post #GirlDad above our photos.

18
Starved

Danny tells me over the phone, "Nah. It's good you're single and don't have a stupid dude over there stressing you out." He says this after three children and a divorce. Evidence, he asserts, he knows of what he speaks.

This was his response to my sharing a sense of being stuck in a holding pattern. Like my father, romance does not yield to the formula. There is no passion in perfection. Nothing authentic in the fear and rejection of flaws. I know this, but still can't seem to unlearn the association. The old me left and the new me hasn't entirely arrived. I'm idled on a stretch of road between them.

A girl's first love is her father, I hear. Because from him she learns to receive care and protection from a man. She knows Daddy will always make things better. Even a failing father isn't too bad in her eyes.

Whether or not the girl grows up to intimately engage with men, she maintains the initial binary image of a male/female relationship imprinted on her psyche—for better or worse. Her father is her first example, her first measuring stick, and if their bond is healthy, she often sets him as an unreachable target.

So many in my generation of our family didn't have fathers. Those cousins born to aunts who had the fortune or foresight to choose dedicated procreation partners had different upbringings than the rest of us. They weren't raised by our grandmother. They shared a paternal bloodline with their siblings. We who were less lucky did not know a stable two-parent household or a consistent co-parenting regime. Then the others, those of us in the subset of this group, did not grow up with two parents at all.

We try to love a father who treats a mother like rotting waste. One who drags her out into a swamp in the middle of the night to fetch water for his car stalled in the street. He is one who re-enters her life only to inflict chaos, before abandoning her and their children again.

There is another father, who douses a mother's food with lighter fluid, physically forces her to take a couple of bites, ignites a cigarette lighter, and tries to pry her mouth open.

There is another, and another—fathers who are but ideas. Whose existence is known but unseen. They leave memories unformed.

A couple of us others sat in the back of a car driven by one of the lucky ones. She does not know our life.

"How do you know what to look for in a man when you've never had a father?" My more than fifteen-years-younger cousin, Aunt Mona's daughter, asked the group. There was an innocence in Dana's voice, a genuine curiosity.

Two generations filled the vehicle. My married cousin and Aunt Niecy, who both maintained healthy relationships with their fathers, sat in the front seats. We were returning to our hotel after a family member's wedding and got to talking about choosing a mate and finding your person.

We talked about how heterosexual women often look for men like their fathers. The topic came up because the bride had just married a man in whom we identified many similarities to her dad. Dana wanted to know what she might do in the absence of such a baseline.

"I think about the same thing," I responded. "I think that's why it took me a while to figure out what I want in a man." To be honest, I'm eternally figuring it out. I know I want someone thoughtful, ambitious, and honest. The rest of the list is fluid. Some days a man having children is a deal-breaker, other days it's fine.

My aunt said she thought I would have used her father, Grandaddy, as the prototype. He was a good man, a good person, and the most consistent male presence in my life. But I didn't establish him as a model, not because I found him unsuitable, but because we didn't have much of a relationship. I didn't know him the way his daughters did.

"Grandaddy was simple," I said. "He just wanted his coffee and paper in the morning, and his dinner at night, and he was content. He didn't argue or ask for much."

My cousin took her eyes off the road for a second to turn and glance at me, a look of confusion spread across her face. "They're all simple," she retorted. "If you come across a man who's difficult and moody, you better run."

"I know that's right!" Aunt Niecy chimed in. Laughter filled the car. She reached back and gave me a playful slap on the leg when I said Uncle Vincent is nothing like Grandaddy, though I didn't mean for it to carry negative connotation. "He wasn't in the beginning, but he is now!" she affirmed.

Their insight was intriguing, how they thought relationships with men to be easy yet worthwhile. I knew it wasn't a coincidence they both felt this way. Still, no one had a solution to satisfy my younger cousin's longing.

———

Love is a young person's game. I wonder where they've all gone, those guys from my twenties who didn't grow weary of working to gain my affection now that I'm more willing to offer it. I want to track them down. I want to call them, call Jason, and say, "I'm ready now. I think." But I suppose one's energy for such pursuits is not infinite.

There are exceptions suggesting I might already be enough. Guys who enjoy me as I am calm my compulsion to become someone else. There is no pretending with them because they hold no idyllic expectation of who I should be. When they let me be quiet, it makes me wish to speak. When they allow me to sit a couch's length away, it makes me want to move closer. Because they care for and consider me in my indifference, the indifference dissipates.

When deeming myself enough, I believe I am more. Affection wasn't normalized for me, but it's only in feigning comfort that it feels most unnatural. Afforded space to unfold, I can. So, I've learned to seek them out, patient partners and perceptive lovers who are in no rush to conquer me. Still, getting here is one thing, staying is another. I'm all in when there are no stakes. When things get serious, I get uneasy and worry the novelty of me might be wearing off. I brace for the end once I care whether it comes. I'm taking the tiniest baby steps. Learning to stop and ask myself if a guy I've grown close to is really behaving differently and pulling away. Or are my insecurities telling me he is? Even if unsure of the answer, I don't stick around to find out.

One chilly fall evening a boyfriend told me he was taking a weekend trip to a cabin in the mountains with his buddies. Later, when he discovered they'd all brought their girlfriends, he asked me to drive up on my own and save him from his third-wheel status. I pictured myself navigating twists and turns along the mountain's edge, alone, in a vehicle not built for the terrain, surrounded by darkness. Suddenly, I was annoyed beyond retrieval. It seemed insensitive of him not to consider me from the start and then ask me to drive unaccompanied through the woods at night and take his arm. But rather than discuss the issue and maybe come to an understanding, I opted for light chatting while he was away, and told him things weren't working out when he returned. We lasted two months.

I called things off with another guy, Chris, after discovering he'd posted an inappropriate comment on an ex's Instagram post. He was admittedly still in love with her. Nevertheless, he promised nothing similar would happen again. He assured me their relationship was dead, unrevivable, and I was the person with whom he was focused on building a future. None of it mattered. I reaffirmed *our* relationship was also over. Except I hung up the phone and wept.

I do more of that now, cry, but never over a man. Chris asked within days of meeting me if I'd be his girlfriend. He said he'd never felt so certain about what he wanted. I didn't make him wait two weeks, like in high school. But I thought it'd be best if we took a little more time to get to know one another. We did, and then we both felt certain.

Chris taught me to ride a four-wheeler and drove across the city to give me a kiss goodbye before traveling out of town. He bought me souvenirs and whether I was at home or work, came straight from the airport to deliver them. He cooked all our meals when I stayed at his place. He opened doors, pumped my gas, washed my car, and tended to me in ordinary ways that felt remarkable. If I called Chris for any reason, at any time, I held no doubt he'd show up. I wanted to have what I had with him always. Then, after about six weeks, I could only hope I'd have it again.

The lump in my throat and pain in my abdomen when I broke up with Chris were new. Even in my agony I realized this was good. Maybe I could care deeply for someone after all, because I could mourn our abrupt separation. It was the forced exit, the departure for which I was unprepared but felt I must make. It cracked me open.

I've ended situationships in response to excessive lying, for demonstrated even if not malicious disregard, and for a myriad of other reasons, justified and not. Discussing even minor concerns with men I've dated never crossed my mind. It wasn't on the table. The solution was always, end it. Expeditiously. If by chance I did muster the vulnerability to frame a conversation around a painful transgression, moving past it and maintaining the entanglement remained a daunting task.

Vegas has not taught me how to love. Not fully. Not unconditionally. But I've been saving up courage to try.

As Dana sits next to me, presenting questions I've always held but never found the nerve or conviction to ask, I realize she is me. We're both working to become who we might be in another life. We're seeking directions to a place we have yet to travel to. Both more curious than we've ever been, we hope to take the hands of the little fatherless girls inside us and lead them to freedom.

We would be different, Dana and I, if we had relationships with our fathers. Without question we would not engage, attach, or partner the same. We would also be different if other elements of our lives were altered. I just know I must face the influence of this one if I am to overcome it. And I want to overcome it. I can't continue carrying baggage with no mercy in its weight.

I really tried. I really aimed to avoid centering the effects of fatherlessness on dealings with men, because unrelated results can be just as impactful. The lost or never-formed sense of security, the erosion of belief, the aversion to extending grace for fear it might be abused, the rigid impulse to exercise control we now have—it all affects how we move through the world.

Still, I've come to accept that there is a correlation. The link between fatherlessness and how daughters associate with not only men but in any intimate relationship is inseverable. It's not the only factor, and how much of a factor it is depends largely on the environment and people around you. Yet, when you come from the unfulfilled expectations of a nuclear family, it is a factor.

I typed *fatherless daughter* into Google. The next word it predicted was *syndrome*. I'd never heard that phrase. The term sent a jolt up my spine. It offended me. Syndrome? They made it sound so dire.

The syndrome, Google says, is *an emotional disorder that stems from issues with trust and lack of self-esteem that leads to a cycle of repeated dysfunctional decisions in relationships with men.*

Not having a father I'm sure has affected me in a manner beyond what I've imagined. Certainly, it manifests in ways I've yet to notice. But I don't fit neatly into the mold set for what is apparently a condition. Neither does Dana.

She and I bucked the patriarchal promiscuity trend commonly pegged as the most prominent indicator of a fatherless daughter. Although I actively try to avoid falling into the societal trap of analyzing women only in terms of sexuality, we remain incessantly measured against male-dominated ideas of how we should behave. Evaluations begin and end with our proximity to what's deemed "ladylike." Women can and do happily, wholly exist outside this manufactured box. Women can and do have sex for pleasure. We can simply enjoy the company of men without it signaling an attempt at soothing daddy issues.

I realize a fatherless girl growing up to chase the male closeness she yearned for is also not uncommon. The pattern has been recorded, discussed, and studied for decades. Dana and I live in stark contrast, however. Not nuns or saints by any means, but not looking for love in the beds of men, either. I suppose it's because we don't even have enough data to make such a correlation. Maybe some part of us doesn't deem it feasible. Or maybe we just don't know what to look for or what to do once we've found it.

Our self-esteem is no less intact than the average adult. It may even exceed the standard. We date, but don't tolerate even hints of poor treatment. We don't carry an insatiable appetite for male attention, craving an intimacy we haven't known or can't get enough of once offered a taste. It's the opposite. We are starved. Starved for meaningful connection. Fasting from our own softness. Searching for misplaced parts of ourselves. The easy parts. The vulnerable parts. The parts unapologetic in seeking to have our intangible needs met. The parts able to ask for help without feeling burdensome. Our challenge is figuring out how to receive love from men and believe the love we receive.

I don't know which side is more damaged, the overindulgent or the malnourished. I'm undecided on which set of broken hearts is easier to mend. But maybe someday, they might talk more about ours.

19

Ordinary Tuesday

I went digging again, two years after Kobe. Not on social media this time but through search engine results. Now a news story about a man who might be my father is spread across the computer screen.

The man in the accompanying image looks how I'd imagine my father to look thirty years removed. Gravity has won the battle with his face. His once high and pudgy cheeks sit lower now, less defined, drooping like sandbags.

Though the article was written in January 2013, the man in the mugshot looks much older than he did in the Facebook photo. Maybe he's using an outdated profile picture, sourced from better days. Perhaps he's presenting himself on social media as he'd like to be seen, as the version of himself he likes most.

The subject of the story shares my father's first and last name. He's wearing a dingy white t-shirt. The crewneck collar, ragged and worn, is stretched well past its normal circumference.

His zodiac sign is Pisces. Like Danny's. Something I learn today because the article details an arrest and includes the suspect's date of birth.

He's homeless, the man in the photo who might be my father—known to frequent local Tennessee businesses. A worker tells the police his panhandling both inside and outside establishments is common. Then one day he ups the ante.

While a crew cleans a car dealership after hours, he sneaks in and nabs multiple sets of car keys. He slips out and presses one of the panic alarms to determine which vehicle it belongs to. The honking horn and flashing lights lead him to the silver SUV he drives off the lot.

Employees at a nearby store know him well. He comes in flashing the fistful of keys, claiming a woman let him drive her car. A clerk watches him leave in the brand-new sport utility vehicle with no license plate or temporary tag, and no woman in sight.

The inevitable occurs.

Now there's this story on the local news website. It includes a name and a picture removing any sliver of room for his denial. The man's mugshot displays an expressionless stare. Though I don't suppose many smile for such a camera, there's something more here. Or something less.

A few scars interrupt the smooth skin of a tired face. There's a blemish beneath an eyebrow. A small knot on his forehead. A set of bags rests beneath his eyes. His hair is cut low, almost bald. The side profile of his mugshot displays more nicks, more little purple marks and scratches.

The man in the photo doesn't look serious. With the corners of his mouth turned downward, he looks sad. He looks exhausted, perhaps more relieved to have lodging for the night than fearful of what it might cost him.

With his mother gone, who's here to be disappointed in him? Who's here to help? Is there anyone to offer refuge from the harsh circumstances of his life? Is there anything tethering him to accountability? I have so many questions.

The system might have set him free days after recovering the stolen vehicle. Free to return to living with no address. Free to resume soliciting patrons and workers for spare change or food outside grocery stores. Free to again receive the demeaning glances and dehumanizing treatment that might make one boast about a stolen vehicle just to garner some respect. I cannot speak on the comparison of captivity to freedom without shelter. I only speculate on which space makes him feel most like Champ.

Even with ample evidence, the burden of proof satisfied, some part of me says I can't know for sure if this man is my father. A fragment of me continues its struggle to make him real again. To see him as a person, not an idea.

I don't know everywhere my father has been or all he's endured. But I do know, now more than ever, his absence wasn't about me. It was about personal struggles and vices and choices that took him places he may or may not have wanted to go.

Hurtful still are the sins of omission. Yet a father's neglect affords you an opportunity to reimagine the relationship as it could have been, as it should have been. It allows you to envision future relationships as they could be, without the barrier of memories overwhelmed by painful hands-on harm.

I hope it might do this for me.

Finding the news article, seeing the picture, and navigating thoughts of his psychological state stirred my empathy for Champ. I wish suffering upon no one, and, in his photo, suffering was apparent. If he would have located me and asked for my help, despite what I make myself believe, I might have run to save him.

———

I suppose we reach for things once ready to hold them. While working at my desk on an ordinary Tuesday, the urge to investigate my lineage overcame me. Not to meet those who rest on the branches of my family tree, but to meet more pieces of myself.

Suddenly it seemed silly to not have a single verifiable detail regarding my paternal genes. Responding "as far as I know" when asked about my ethnicity struck me as ridiculous.

Before the moment passed, I made my very first inquiry into ordering an at-home DNA kit. I read through a bunch of data and put a package into my online cart. But unsure if I wanted the information badly enough to spend $100 to obtain it, I didn't checkout. I closed the web page and went on about my business.

Days went by, and the urge remained. It wasn't a random, fleeting desire, but continued to live beyond its initial appearance. Some part of me coveted the knowledge for reasons unknown to the other parts.

I'm now certain I don't care enough to drop $100 on an ancestral analysis, yet I spend it anyway. I go back to the website and order the kit for the slice of me that has grown curious, even though I'm confident learning more about my origins won't fundamentally change who or where I am.

A small box arrives a week later. I tear it open with trembling hands and examine the contents. A sponge, saliva collection tube, plastic baggie, return packaging, and instructions are spread across my kitchen counter.

Everything I planned for the evening is put on pause. I'll cook dinner later and skip the gym altogether. I'm excited, anxious to solve a mystery. Within the span of one hour, I collect my sample, seal it in the packaging, drive to a post office, and drop it in the mail.

My sense of urgency is exhilarating to the point of startling.

I want to know what's inside me of which I am unaware. Have I lied to myself all these aloof years? Days after shipping the saliva-filled tube, I get an email. *Your sample has been received.* My pulse thumps in my throat. Soon I'll know something definitive. I'll have information about myself I've never had before.

They always give you the worst-case scenario is the thought I think after reading my results will come in six to eight weeks. I'm right.

About three weeks later, I get another email. There is again a throbbing throughout my upper body. It slows to an almost standstill as I read the message.

We're so sorry, but we're having some trouble and haven't been able to process your DNA sample. We apologize for the inconvenience. Confirm your replacement DNA kit, and we'll send you a new one. Once we receive your sample, we'll process it as soon as possible.

I drop into some mixture of discouragement and frustration. Maybe I've had it right all along. Knowledge of familial history, and the however unlikely potential of connecting with my father's relatives, isn't meant to occupy space in my life experience.

Maybe I'm pushing an issue best left alone. It's possible I've been saved from something in my not knowing. This ignorance may be bliss. Or maybe this is a test to see if I really am ready for the big reveal.

I return to the email and click the button to confirm my free replacement kit. I wait. Again. It comes.

There's no sponge this time, but a funnel and a few other altered details I suppose are to ensure more accurate collection. Like before, I immediately gather and ship my sample. What's a few more weeks after a thirty-year delay? Although only now am I held in expectation.

Your results are in, an email subject line tells me one morning about a month later. I'm surprised by the message, almost like I'd forgotten what I'd done. Instead of opening the email, I place my phone back on the nightstand and grab the book sitting next to it. After reading for twenty minutes, I close the book and roll over to close my eyes, still not fully awake. At least, not awake enough to process the heaviness awaiting me.

A weird dream comes to me during the ten-minute power nap. It gives me a headache. I pick up my phone again to check social media, play Wordle, and do anything but open the email. Stretched across my bedroom floor now, I complete my morning routine with a few yoga poses while listening to a podcast on *The Law of Attraction.*

I'm hungry. To the kitchen I go to fill my kettle with water and make breakfast. I carry my green tea, gluten-free waffle and turkey bacon to a tray positioned in front of my couch and turn on the television.

Halfway through my meal, I get a text message. *Your DNA results are in!* The exclamation point means the notification is to be exciting. *In case you didn't know, in case you didn't get our eariler email,* I imagine is the text's tone. There's a link. I don't click it, returning my attention to the TV and my breakfast.

I'm . . . afraid. Once anxious to know, I'm now fearful of what I might find. What if Champ is connected to my family tree and sees I've been added? What if he thinks I'm trying to find him? What if he or his relatives attempt to contact me?

After I've done all I can possibly do to stall, I open the email.

It's the moment you've waited for. Your DNA results are ready. Now, it's time to discover what it is about your DNA that makes you uniquely you.

I tap the clickable button of no return: *Explore your DNA results.*

The site takes a few seconds to load. I watch a wheel spin in the middle of the screen for what registers as much longer.

Finally, there's a pie chart breaking down my ethnicity estimate. It's color-coded for easy analyzing.

I'm not overwhelmingly anything. The chart shows I'm thirty percent something, eighteen percent something else, with smaller percentages scattered across the thirteen world regions to which my DNA has been linked. The most dominant regions are the Ivory Coast, Ghana, Nigeria, and Cameroon. My remaining lineage falls within Ireland, Scotland, England, Sweden, and a host of other territories that don't include any in South or Latin America.

I've been right, mostly. The guy and all those others who were certain I was of Latin descent were wrong. Or were they?

Back when I checked the in-progress results of the failed first test, I saw something different. While processing, the available data had my DNA spread across places like Mexico, Columbia, and Chile. That this test was determined inaccurate has me questioning the validity of both.

I navigate to the section labeled DNA Matches. Of the 1,000 individuals listed, I share more than eight percent DNA with only one person. The strongest match is a first cousin I grew up with. Everyone else is considered a very distant relative, fourth, fifth, and sixth cousins.

I want to cry.

I want to cry and don't know why.

I don't know what I was expecting, what I might have secretly hoped to find.

Not my father.

But there's no one here with whom I share a more immediate bloodline. This makes me sadder than not knowing my heritage ever has.

The DNA test, especially factoring in the initial botched results, provides me no answers, just more evidence of not having any. And I guess somewhere along the way I've decided I'd like to belong to someone. I'd like to have people. I thought I might find someone who'd like to find me.

20
Tell Me A Story

I've been hurt, cut deep, by significant others. A lover left me. I've been a version of myself I do not recognize nor like—asking for explanations, waiting for a phone to ring, writing revenge blogs, social media stalking a past partner's current whereabouts. Crying, crying, spying. I've allowed someone to turn me from a woman of substance to . . . this.

My line between independence and loneliness has blurred. This tells me I'm growing. That I've even put myself in a position to be discarded means my walls are weakening. Now to find a healthy balance between letting people in and letting them exploit the access. I've somehow let these new men assume a manipulative adaptation of my old role in relationships—unsure, unforgiving, guarded, but pretending to be none of these things. At least I was upfront, swift with my shield! I suppose that's what I get, huh? That's my karma. We attract who we are and the person I once was has been flocking to me. You'd think I'd see them coming.

Irrespective of how these more consequential connections end, each has helped me learn this critical lesson. Not to save room for love, but that love *is* the room. You build everything else inside.

Having dinner with Dana for the first time since our after-wedding car conversation a year prior, we caught each other up on current events. "Letting myself get close to people, it's teaching me more specifically what I want in a partner. What draws me to them." I shared my evolving perspective. How I'm all in on openness, but still struggling with asking anyone to do anything for me.

"People *want* to help you," Dana said. My little big cousin, wise beyond her years. Others once used these same words to describe me. I suppose growing up in neglect makes you grow up faster. Your thought process matures sooner. You develop a sensitivity and hone instincts necessary to protect yourself. Plus, any delusions you held about human behavior and how things work were long ago shattered. Early heartbreak teaches lessons whether you're ready to learn or not.

If lacking experience in the area, your inner voice heckles you when asking for help. It can be difficult to hear logic over its screams of *needy* and *weak*. If you manage to tune it out and ask anyway, then comes worry. What if the request is denied? This outcome sends people like me down a dark tunnel of rejection and reinforced certainty that we are uncared for.

Dana assured me people want the opportunity to support every aspect of my life, from achieving my goals to completing everyday tasks. They want me to let them be of service. "That's your trauma telling you otherwise." We finished dinner, and for the rest of the night, I believed her.

———

My belief is tested when I go to pick up two patio chairs purchased online from Target. The outdoor furniture won't fit into
my sports sedan. The store employee and I try everything, shoving the chairs into the back seat, front passenger seat, and the
trunk.

"Do you have another car?" he asks.

"No," I chuckle. I do alright but does the kid think I'm
wealthy? Maybe he just thinks I might be married or otherwise
have someone at home.

"It's not going to fit," he says, defeated, sweating through his
red polo shirt. "It's just not. The legs are too wide. I'm sorry. We
can hold the chairs here if you want to come back with a bigger
car."

"Thank you," I say. "Let me see if I can find someone."

The only person I know with an SUV is Julien, the guy
I've just started dating. He's French and still learning to speak
English. This makes him vulnerable by default. He must con-
verse carefully and honestly to deliver his message because he
doesn't have the words to be coy. This forces me to be vulnerable, too. I must stare at his mouth and look directly at him
when we talk so he can stare at mine. If I turn away, one of us
will miss something.

Julien says, "make love" instead of "have sex." He rolls the
letter *r* in his speech and skips *h* altogether in some words and
doesn't use contractions and of all the voices I've heard, his is
my favorite.

He doesn't possess the cultural nuance to play it too cool,
and conveys feelings exactly as felt. "I was angry but also sad,"
frames one recount. "Sometimes, I would wake in the morning
and there would be little water in my eyes. Almost like, how do
you say . . . cry?" frames another.

I must be patient. What I can say in seconds takes Julien an
entire minute. He stops to use Google Translator when he gets

stuck, puts his forefinger up and says "I'm sorry" before pulling out his phone. I await the completion of his sentence. "No worries."

It's refreshing, his unabashed sincerity. That he would trust me enough to find language for his innermost thoughts digs down into me. It pulls to the surface a desire to protect, to preserve his perception of me as someone with whom he can share his secrets.

Julien lives across town and is always tired because he's a pastry chef who wakes up at three a.m. every morning. I sit in my car contemplating whether to ask him to meet me at Target or return the chairs for a refund. Ten minutes and a million possibilities later, I send him a text.

I tell Julien the scenario and how I hate to ask him but can think of no other option. He's willing to peel himself from the couch and make the drive right away. It releases my apprehension and that is enough to make me comfortable waiting because I know he will come. We agree to handle it tomorrow.

The next day we meet at Target, retrieve the chairs, and take them back to my place. I explain how difficult it was for me to ask him for help. "Why?" he asks. "Either I can do it, or I cannot."

Sounds so simple. Must be how normal brains think. They don't take the word *no* personally or as an indictment of their worth.

Julien grew up without his father too. We bond over the mutual understanding of what it's like to feel you aren't good enough for the people who created you—to the point where you can no longer take efforts to repair severed ties and instead yield to the damage.

Though our experiences as a boy and a girl without a father differ, we're alike in the most paralyzing ways. We both find it difficult to hold positive perceptions of people. Both have often taken the path of most resistance, concluding it is easier to struggle in private than risk unfulfilled or reluctantly fulfilled requests for support. We are late bloomers in the field of love, novices who in our thirties only began developing. Trusting love is its own beast, one we've yet to offer absolute embrace. We historically leave before we are left.

We will leave each other better, maybe? Hopefully. Because aloneness is easier when it's all you know. Having tasted life on the other side, I now know something different. I understand things I'd never understood. Like the desire to spend every free moment with someone for no other reason than to be near them. How quickly chemistry can spark a fire. I understand the fuss about physical intimacy. I like it here, and don't ever want to go back.

Maybe Julien and I will see glee as more than distraction from gloom. For me, it is enough to see each other. I show him my prettiest scars, and still, he doesn't look at me as a girl with daddy issues in need of fixing. He looks at me like someone who picked that girl up and carried her as best she could with what she had.

"Tell me a story," Julien says while my head rests heavy on his chest. The words vibrate through my left ear.

"You tell *me* a story," I say. "In French."

He pauses. "But you will not understand."

I encourage him to try me.

"C'est l'histoire d'un petit cochon," he starts, and waits for me to interpret. *Hmmm* . . . I think before admitting I have no idea what it means.

"I said, this is a story about a little pig." We realize the futility of this activity and surrender our minds to slumber. When we sleep, our bodies, intertwined like pretzels, transcend dialect.

If I could describe who I might envision myself to be had I grown up with a father, I would describe who I am with Julien.

Gentler, more open, naked and unashamed. I want him to know love the way I once wanted to know love and have come around to wanting to know it again. I want him to trust. I want him to know his existence is not a burden, that some people do show up, back their words with actions, and are who they claim to be. I want us to be children again, who we were in our innocence untainted by cruelty.

Though he did not ask me to, I've assumed the role of nurturer that remains vacant in my life, for him. A few dates in, he texts me a picture of teeth the dentist office sent him without explanation. I call and tell the receptionist I'm his partner, so they'll give me basic information to help make his appointment. I explain to the barber how he'd like his hair cut. I volunteer to take him places and show him things he's never seen. And when his face lights up with amazement at the vastness of the Hoover Dam or the wonders of our red mountains, it fills me with every form of delight.

It's supposed to be me though. *I've* longed to know how nurture and protection feel. *I've* wanted to reclaim the lost emotional safety of a parentally complicated adolescence. Never have I envisioned myself doing more creating than occupying such a space.

I realize maybe it's not only the acceptance of adoration I've missed or craved, but the offering as well. I've needed to learn how to give perhaps more than receive—and who knew the giving could be as gratifying?

We each speak to the child inside the other, corroborating their evidence. I assure Julien of things he must have waited a lifetime to hear. "It wasn't your fault." His eyes glaze at the affirmation.

In seeing the child inside him, I see the one inside me. I think back to when she was tricked into getting on The Demon roller coaster at Six Flags. Life has mirrored that experience. I haven't always known what I was getting into. I've twisted and turned, been lifted into the air and dropped back down to earth. I've closed my eyes and looked away when afraid, until I could figure out what was going on and felt safe enough to bear witness to the unfolding. It's been scary. But again, just like The Demon, the scariest parts, the parts I thought would break me clean in two, were over before I knew it.

Lord, if it hasn't been rough at times, though. If it hasn't been spirit-crushing and essence-numbing. Yet here we are, me and that kid. On the other side of it all. Though we know more inevitably awaits. There is always more. More life, more loss, more ache. No matter. This is not a circumstance to avoid or dread. Because I also know now when it passes, as it all does, most instances will be like when The Demon returned me to the ground intact. I'll smile and say, "Man, that wasn't nothing."

I aim to again be the little girl in the window, wearing her best outfit and brightest smile, trusting people to show up for her. Not because they will, but because I deserve to believe I am worth showing up for. I look at her, the child inside me, face-to-face. I see her eyes welling with water, her cheeks flushing with regret, her fists balling, and her heart hardening. I push my face against hers and say, "It's okay."

21
It's Okay

I know you haven't a single childhood memory of being held while crying. Not one. You remember your tears being met with annoyance or indifference. Sometimes dismissive laughter. Even sometimes anger. Adults would tell you to stop crying or they'd "give you something to cry about."

You stuffed your emotions so far down, tears ceased flowing in the presence of others altogether. You grew ashamed to express sadness because no one seemed to care. It made you not trust people with your vulnerability. You couldn't depend on anyone to be there when you needed them for fear they would disappoint and leave you—not just alone, but broken. You hated it.

Resentment occupied the space where sorrow would otherwise reside. You were angry. Always. At everyone in your household. Their presence you either ignored or met with contempt.

If something or someone somehow managed to evoke tears, you shed them behind closed doors. You screamed into pillows.

Anything to avoid the mortifying circumstance of another human witnessing your pain.

But remember when we lost control at Grandma's funeral? When everyone went to the cemetery, we stood staring at her casket as the workers lowered it into the ground. The grief and disbelief almost brought us to our knees.

When we sniffled and sobbed—more in the days following her death than in years, we thought the worst was over. Then came the funeral. And the finality of the cemetery.

Our response to the devastation was just as jolting as the devastation itself. It was a loud bawling. An ugly cry. In front of everyone, we stood there alone with clenched hands, wailing and shaking while the casket continued dropping Grandma into her eternal resting place. We stood on this island of anguish for a pocket of forever.

Exposed.

Uncomforted.

As usual.

Head down, we hoped no one would notice. This posture was all we could think of to draw less attention to our unraveling. Then, a set of arms wrapped around our shoulders from behind.

Cousin Junior. He whispered words that released our already struggling floodgates.

"It's okay."

No one had ever told you this before. Never was your sadness validated or soothed. No one had ever held you while you were crying.

We turned toward Junior and fell onto his shoulder. We cried louder. Uglier.

Junior squeezed tighter. "It's okay. It's okay," he just kept saying. He said it until we conceded.

It's okay.

It's okay to cry and be vulnerable and let people see you hurt. It's okay to sit with and express pain. Your pain matters.

The adults who failed to instill this belief in you simply didn't know how to do such a thing, or even that they should. Their lives were predicated on survival. They had to dry their eyes, pick themselves up and keep moving or die. So, they expected the same from you.

People can't give you things they don't have. It doesn't mean they don't want to give those things to you. It doesn't mean they don't care.

The effort Mommy put into doing your hair and preparing your outfits every morning, was love. The way she made every Christmas magical, was love. Her smashing whole bananas into the pancake batter and putting cinnamon and raisins in the oatmeal because she knew you liked each made that way, was love. Love was even sending you and Danny to stay with Grandma for long stretches while she rebuilt herself.

She didn't give up. She came back from a place not everyone returns from, and assumed the responsibility of two parents. Mommy is a miracle. Therefore, so are you.

I want you to let people hold you. Let people in. And please, don't apologize for your tears.

You didn't experience it until that day at the cemetery, but I want you to remember how protected you felt in the arms of your cousin versus how weak and exposed you felt when standing there alone.

Support is good. It's also available. I promise, people want to love and show up and be there for you.

Something as gentle as an embrace at the perfect moment is divine. You should welcome it more often. Not just at funerals.

As resilient as you are, I want you to let those well-intentioned help carry your heart in its heaviest hours.

I'm proud of you for going it alone when you felt that you must. You are so brave. You survived. You persevered while broken without breaking others.

I wish for you, rest. Peace. Joy. You stood in the rain because you didn't trust the sun. Your greatest act of courage will now be to let people give you shelter.

It's okay.

Acknowledgments

Meeting my friends has been one of my life's greatest gifts. My friends taught me how to trust. They taught me how to show up—how to love and be loved in many different ways. Thank you, Kim, Iris, Kasey, and Timika, for being my family.

I adore my brother's three children. My eldest niece came into my life when I was at a fork in the road. Her innocence and adoration steered me toward a softer version of myself. Thank you, my dear niece, for our relationship. My world is better because you're in it.

Thank you to my brother, my first best friend. I'm afraid to consider the added turns my childhood might have taken, and how it would have affected me, if I'd been forced to endure it alone. I love you. Come back to us.

I hate that it took me so long to recognize my mother's struggles and how miraculous it was that she was around to be a mother at all. Yet, I am happy I got to this place while she's still here for me to say, thank you. Thank you for doing the best you could with what you had. You are appreciated.

Every guy I've ever dated has helped prepare me for my person. You all helped me grow in some area. Even if you are not spoken of favorably here, know that I am thankful for the time we spent together. I don't regret any of it and wouldn't change a thing.

Thank you to everyone who has read my work and supported my endeavors. Lorinda Toledo, my first writing coach, you changed the course of my career by being so generous with your time and wisdom. I am forever grateful. To my friend, Evan, who never tires of reading and supporting and encouraging, I cannot find words sufficient to express what you've meant to me. You are a beautiful human the Randolph MFA program is lucky to have.

Versions of chapters and sections of this book first appeared in *Bellevue Literary Review*, *North American Review*, and *68to05*. To every editor who believed in my work enough to publish it, thank you, not the least of which is Michael Charney at Riddle Brook Publishing. We started with a completely different manuscript. *Daddy's Little Stranger* would not have become what it is if you had not pushed and challenged me every step of the way. It would not have become the story I am so proud of today.

Thank you to everyone who has ever meant anything to me. You know what they say, "blame my head, not my heart" if I have neglected to mention you. This is not the extent of my acknowledgements, only where I'll stop, for now.

About the Author

Acamea Deadwiler is a memoirist and essayist who received critical acclaim from *Publishers Weekly* for her book, *Single That*. She has been featured by the *New York Post*, *Cosmopolitan*, *Bustle*, and the FOX television network, among other media outlets. Acamea is also a TEDx speaker. Currently residing in Nevada, she holds a master's degree from Valparaiso University and is a fellow in the MFA program at Randolph College.